AF587721

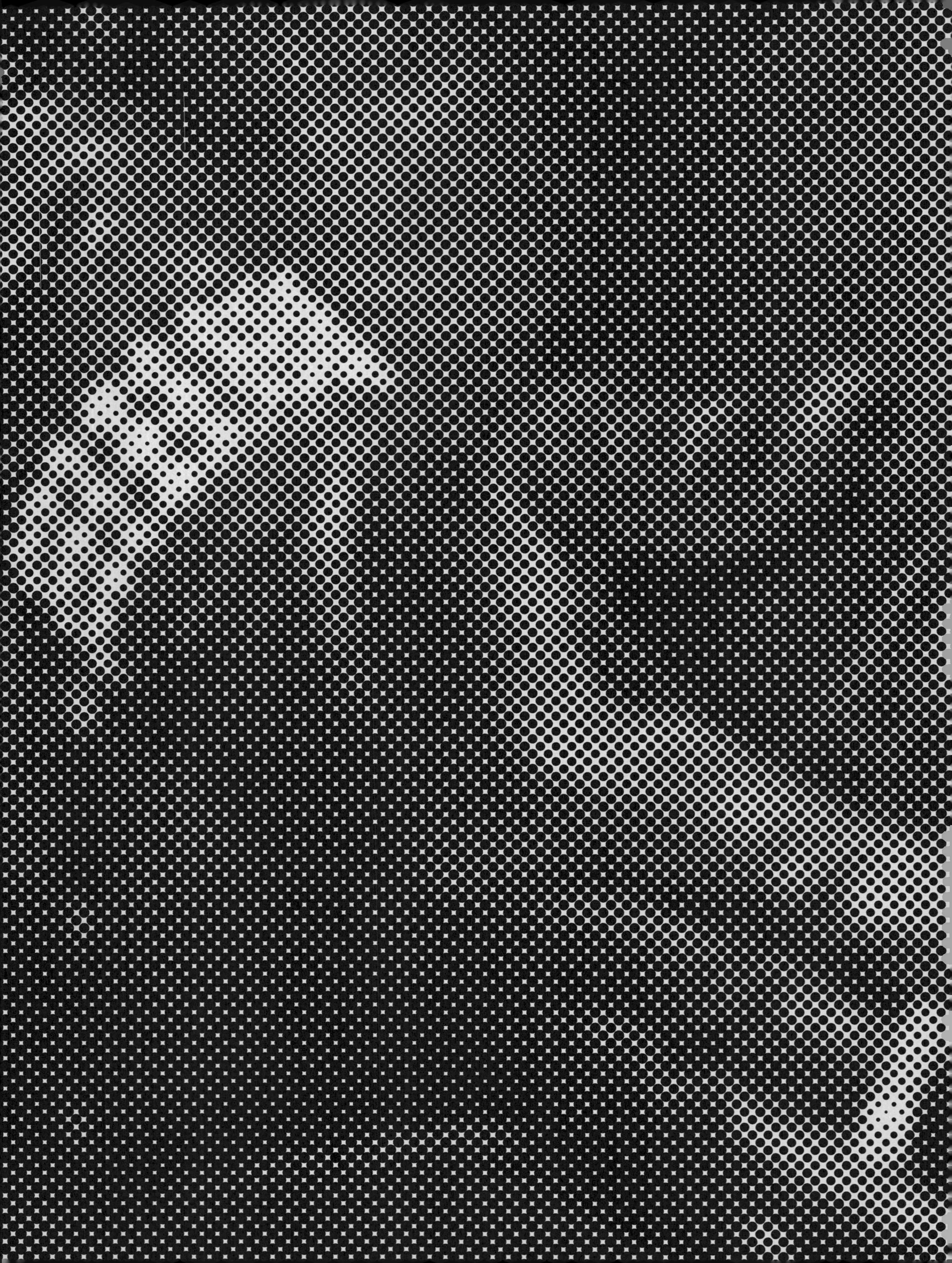

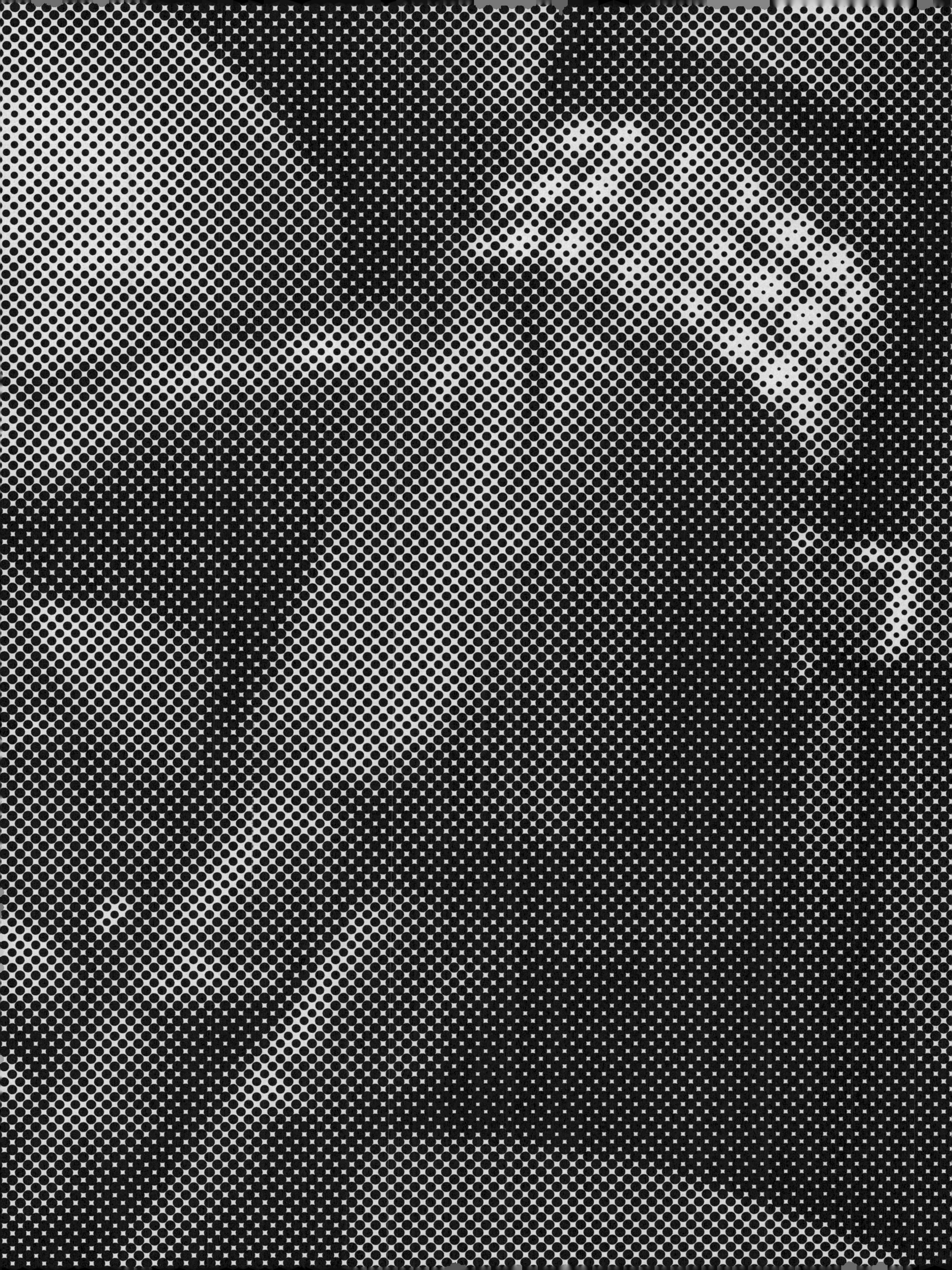

FOREWORD

Over the past three years, I have interviewed and photographed female sex workers, women who choose to make their living as dominatrices, switches, and slaves in the BDSM (Bondage and Discipline, Dominance and Submission, Sadism and Masochism) and fetish community.

The women portrayed are of different ethnicities and come from a wide variety of cultural backgrounds. They often live in the present and think little of their long-term futures. Most are single, but some have relationships. Some are poised, whereas others appear very vulnerable. Many operate honestly and autonomously, although some remain in the sex industry for lack of an alternative. It is these nuances of conviction and inner conflict that interest me.

I wanted to represent the personal narratives of these women and their reasons for choosing this profession, as well as the question of how they view their lives within the sex industry. Their anonymous histories appear alongside their portraits as text, juxtaposed with found footage appropriated from online resources.

During my meetings with the women, I sensed that they tend to live their entire working lives as if on stage. There was an ongoing power play between us; I kept wondering why they agreed to be photographed.

Is it about being remembered? Is it vanity? Did they see me as a potential client? What difference would it have made if I were a woman doing this project? My role remained unclear to the subjects, for whom the camera seemed to offer some kind of salvation – a false promise inherent to photography.

Max Eicke
2016

max eicke

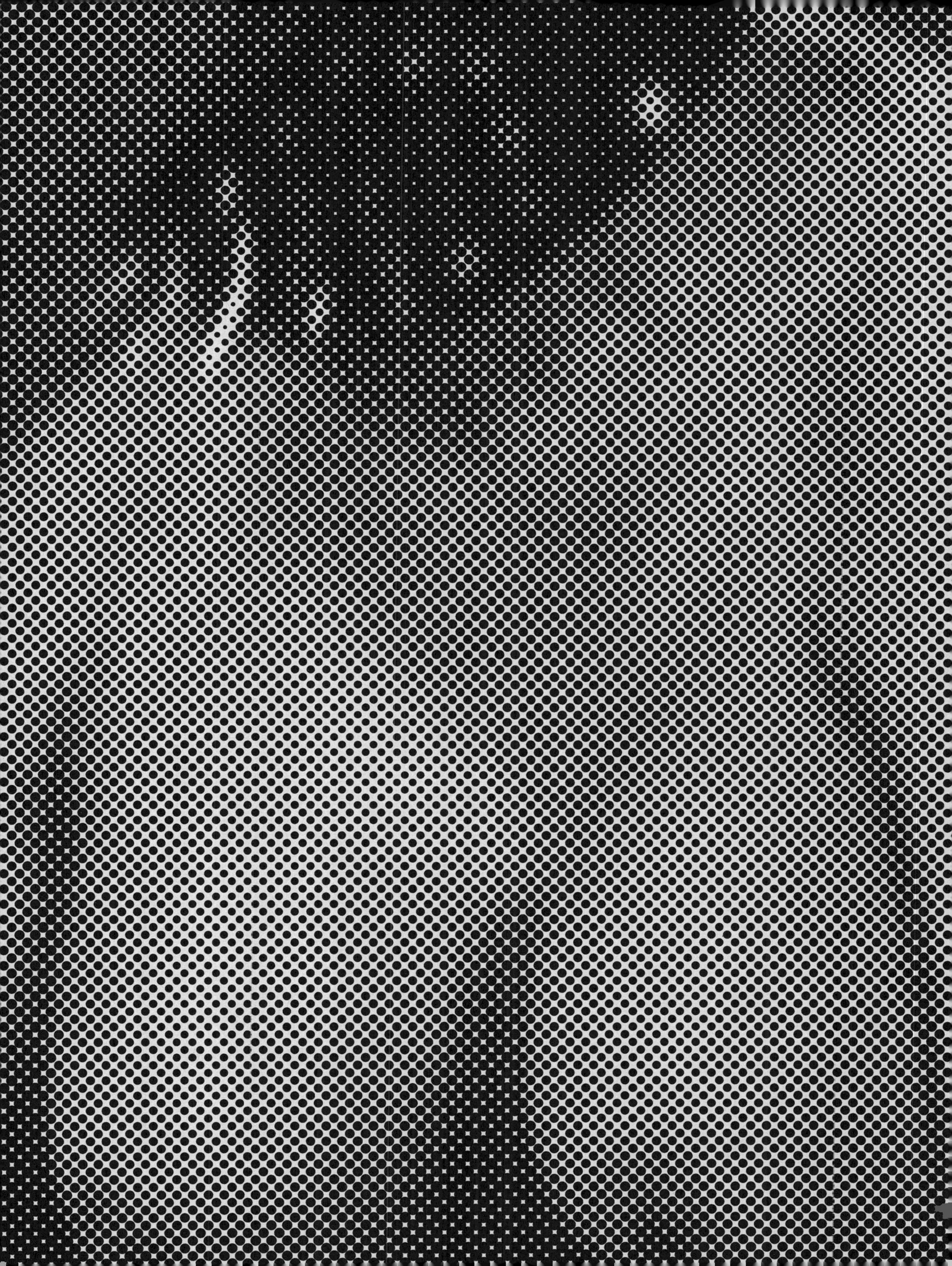

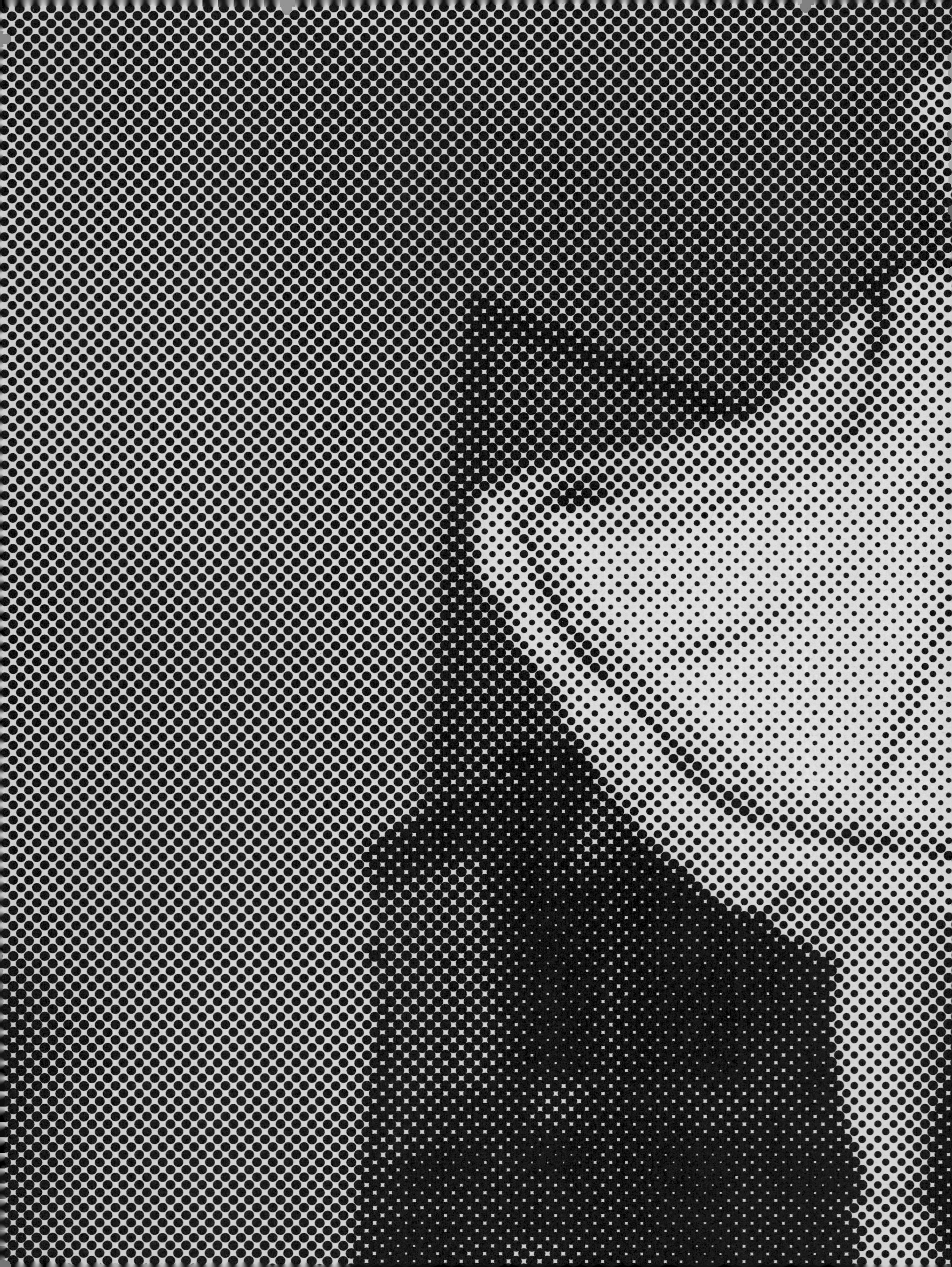

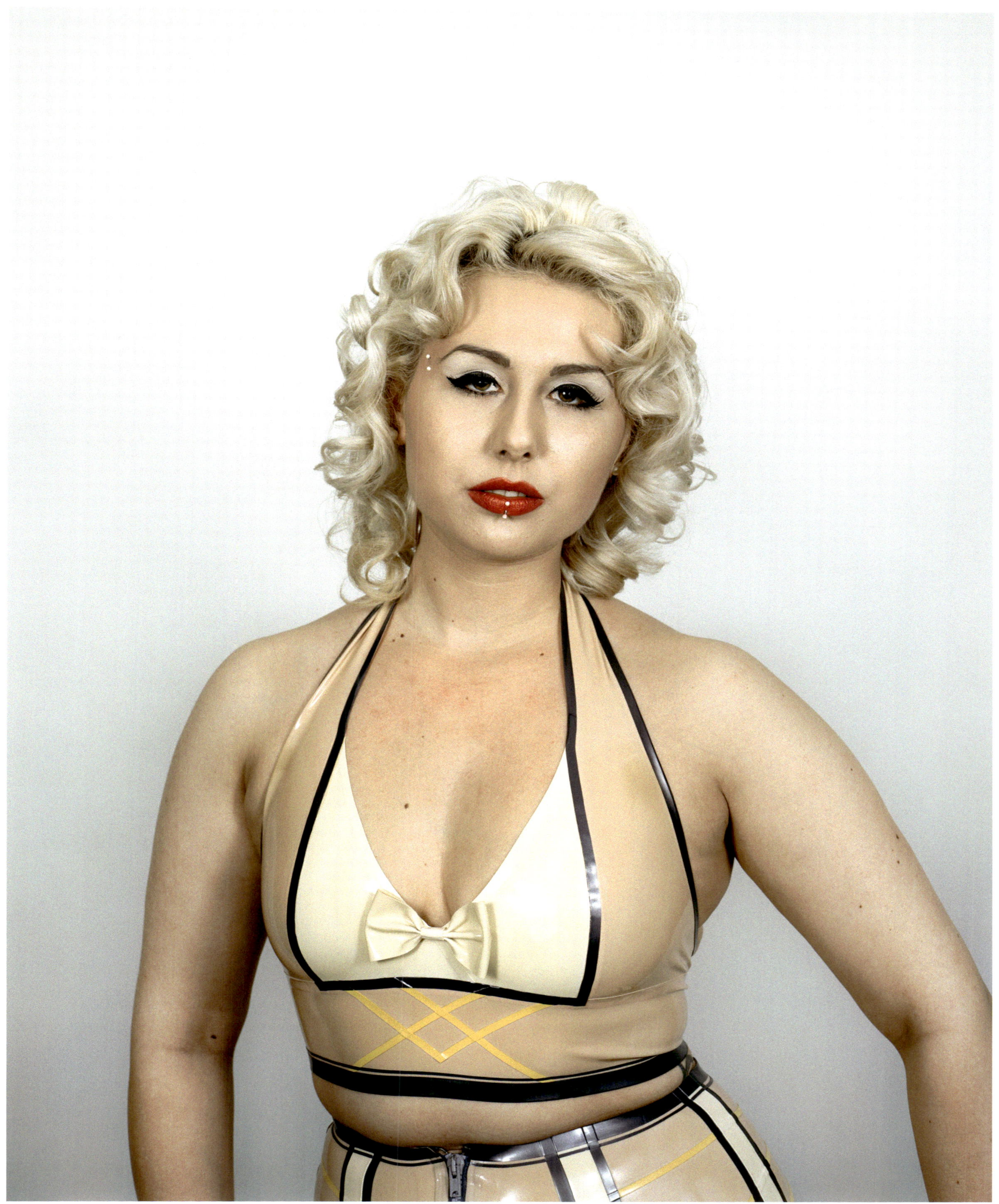

ELIZABETH GARDEN · Berlin, 2013

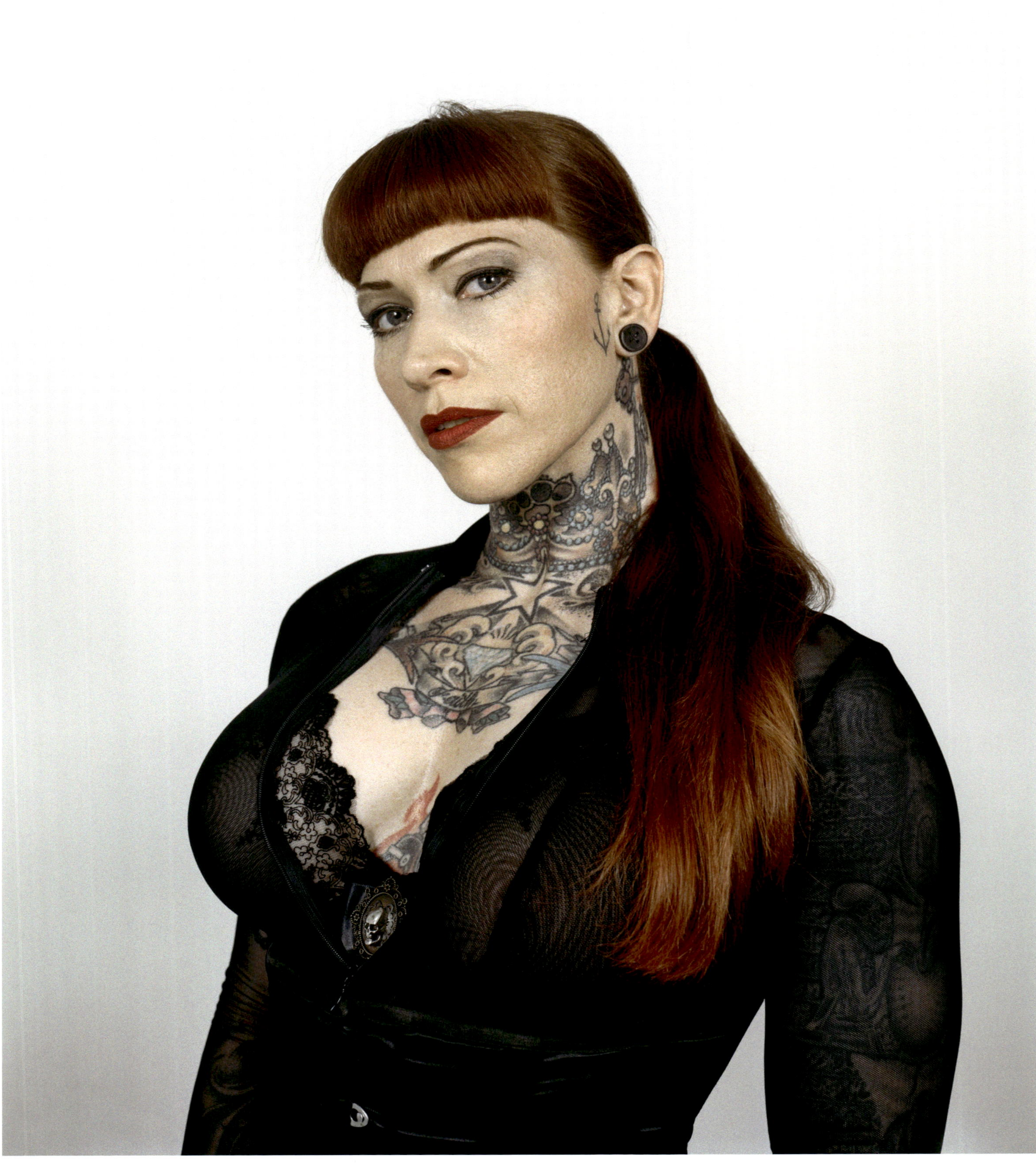

LADY ALEXA · Frankfurt, 2016

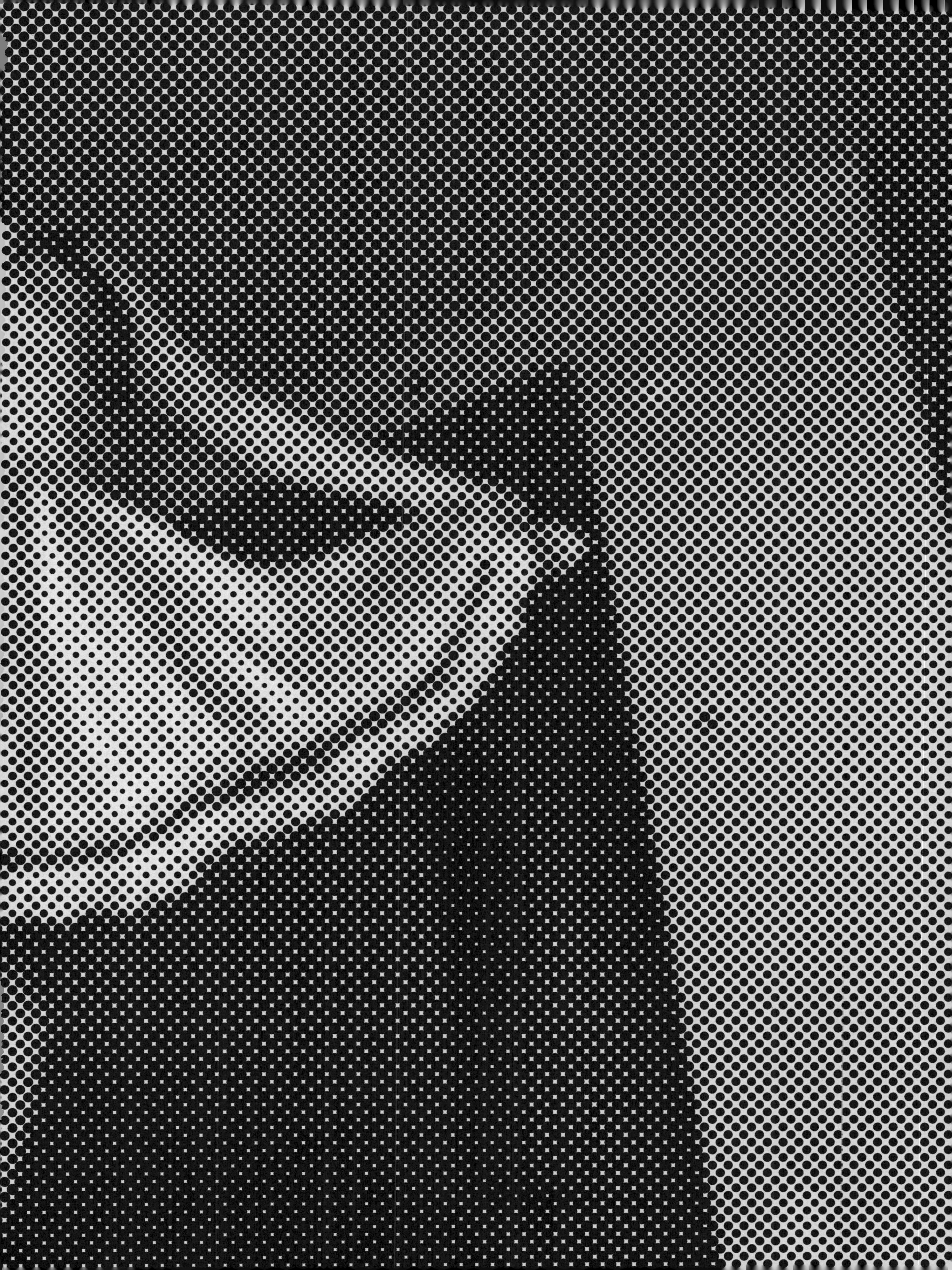

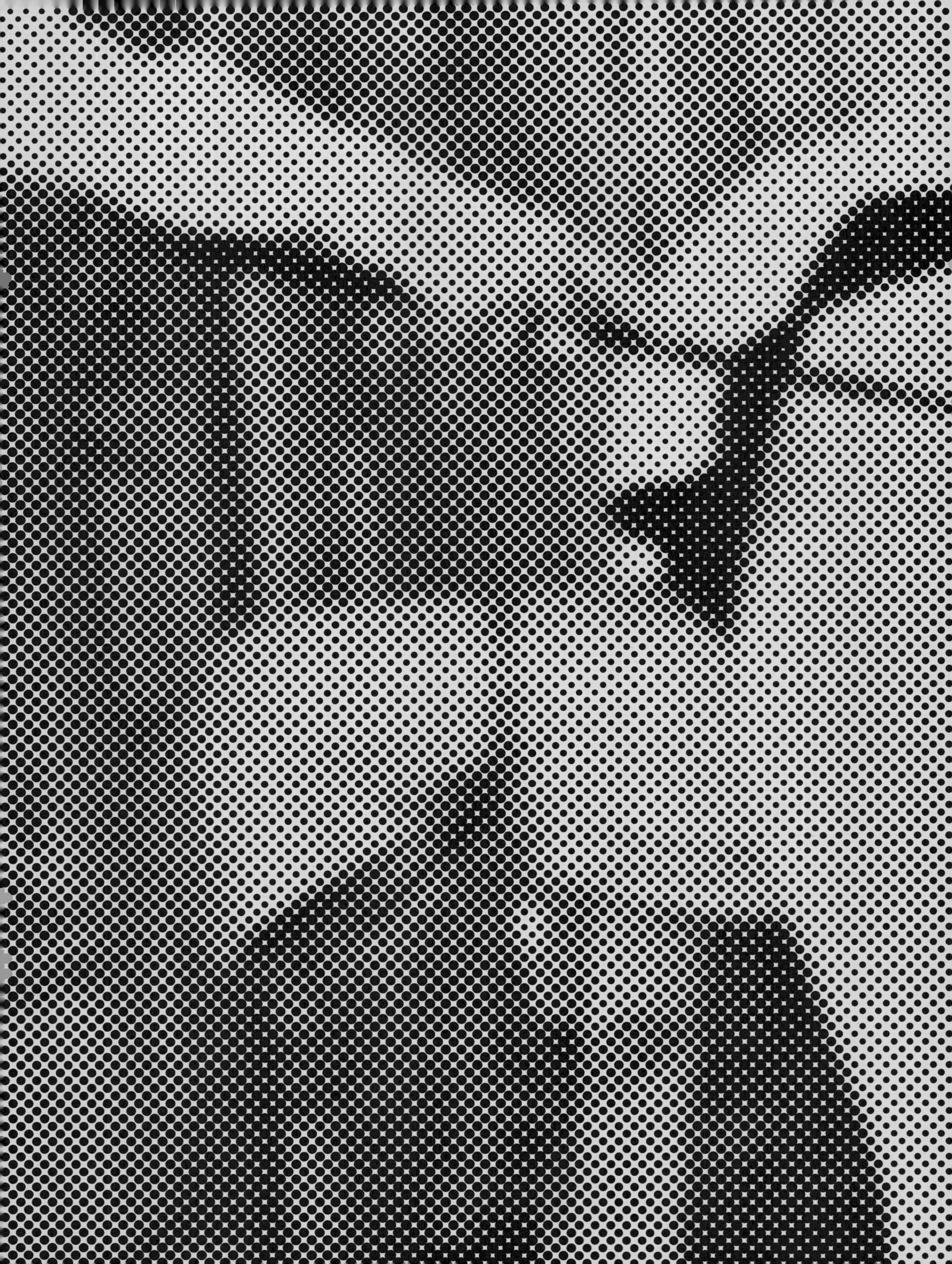

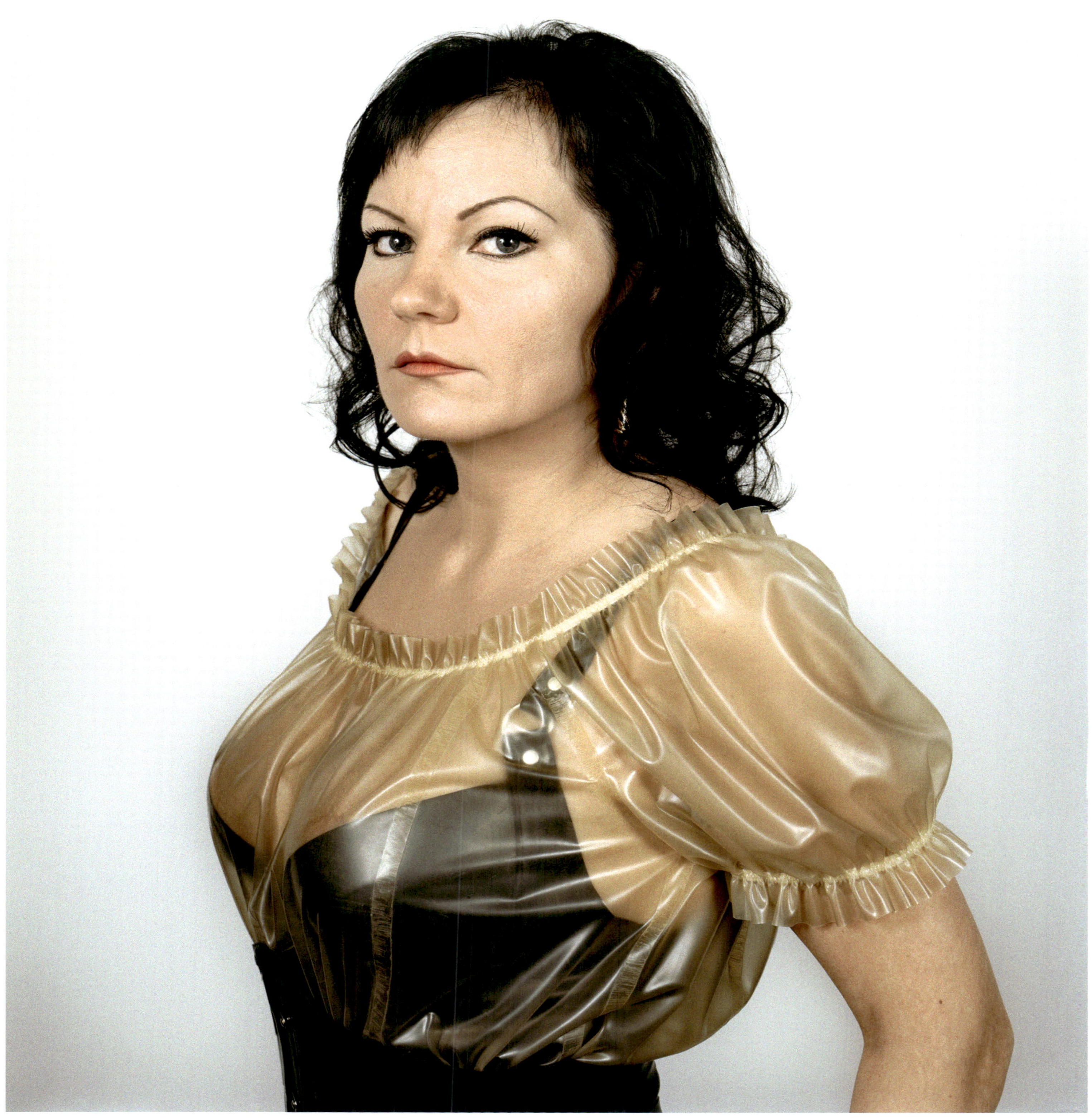

LADY LUCY · Berlin, 2014

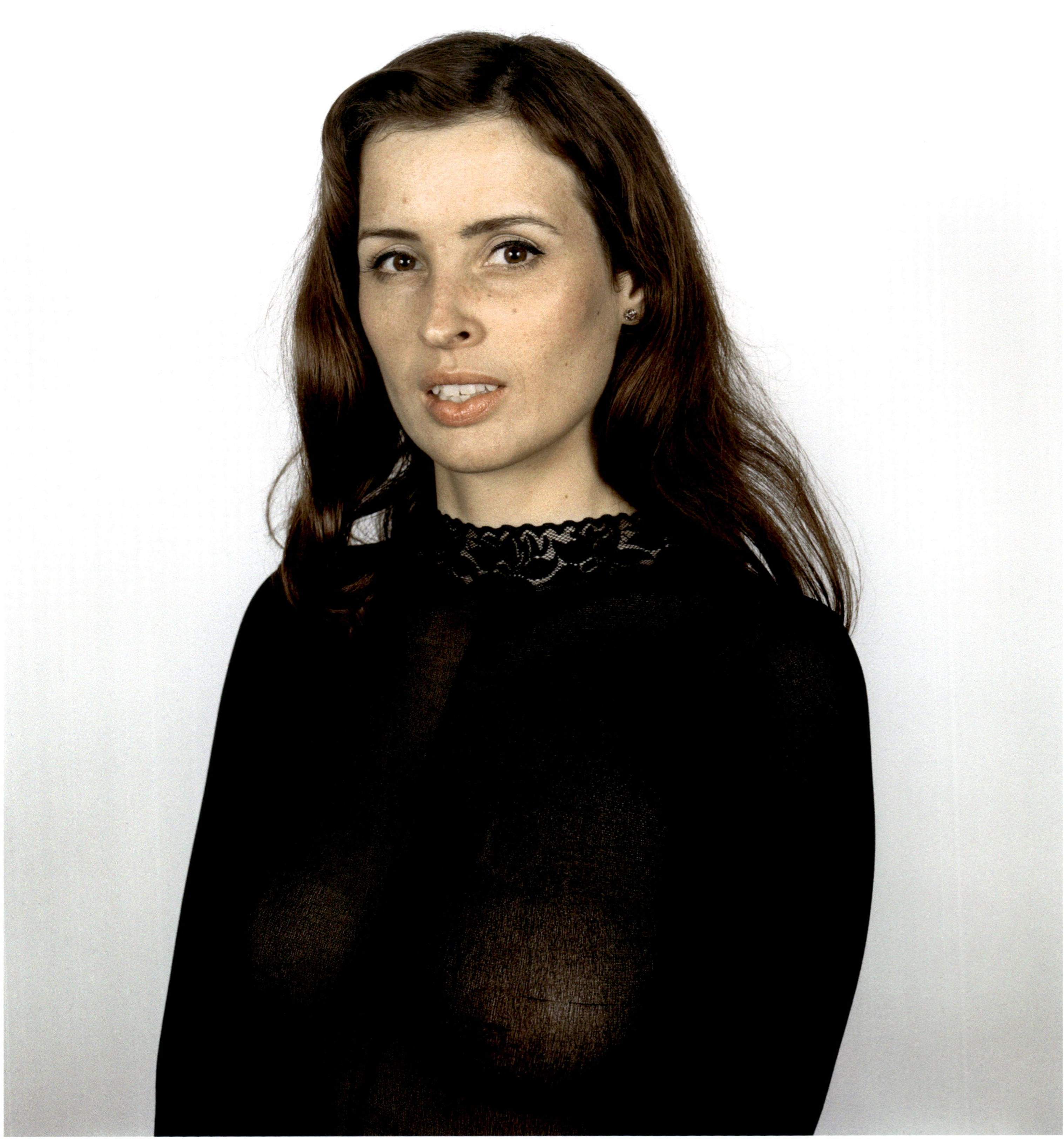

FROLLEIN LINA · Frankfurt, 2016

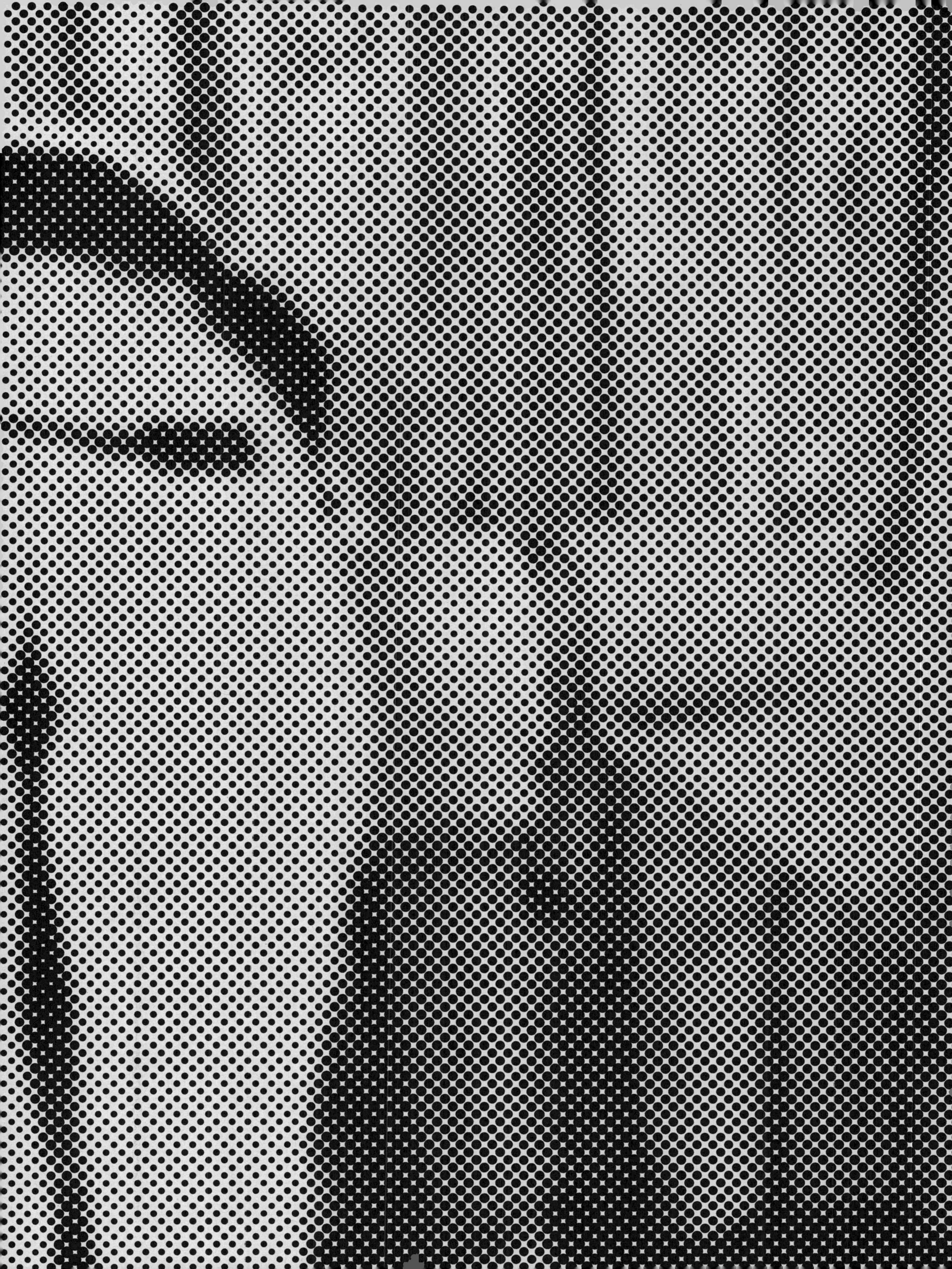

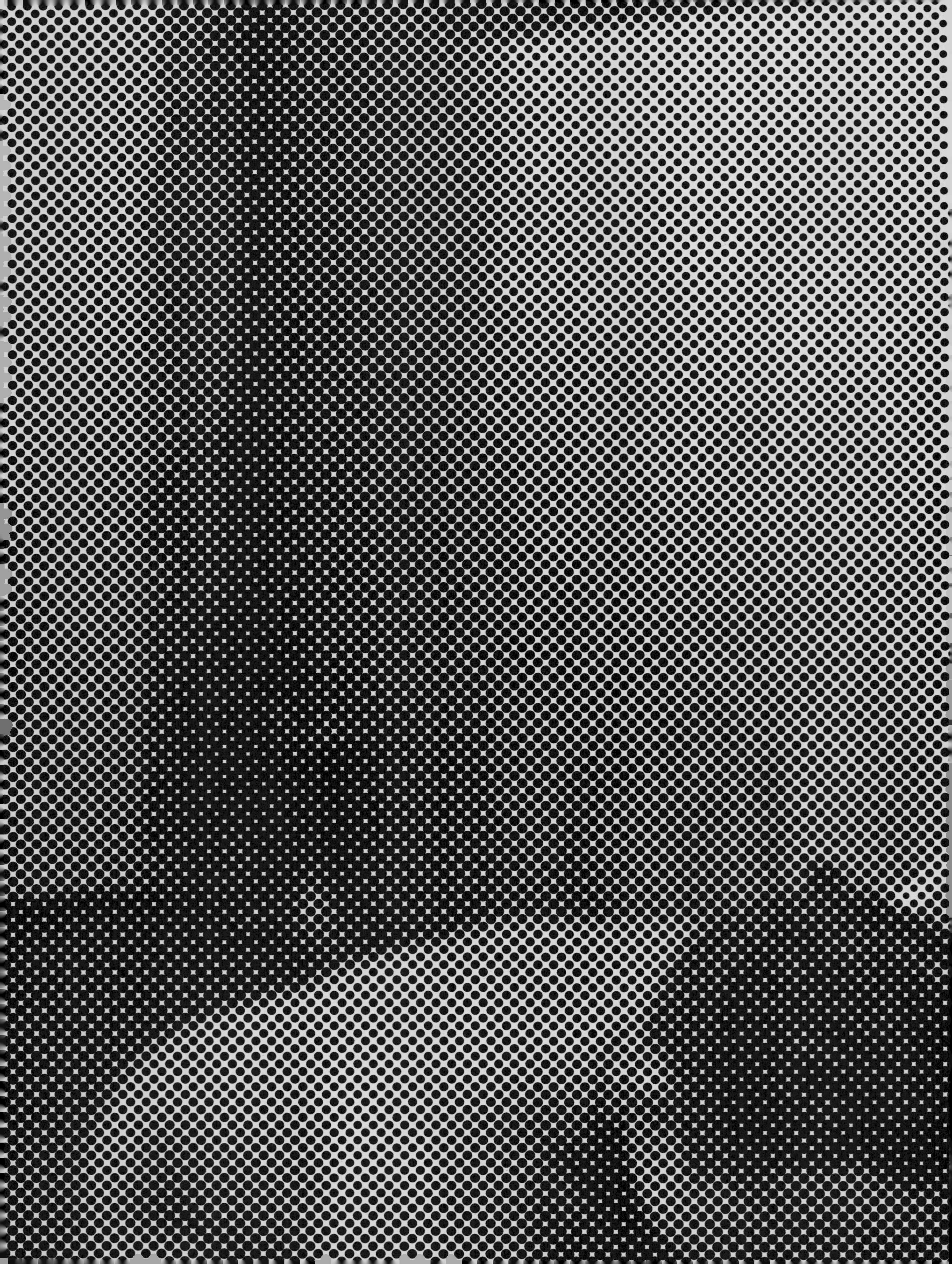

'This is the first job in which I don't sell myself. Before, I always fought to be able to function in society as myself, the way I am, and, in doing so, I sold myself. But I don't have to function. I'm good just the way I am.'

'At some point after I had already started working, I thought to myself, this is me. I can tell stories about how, as a small child, I dissected snails and did other things and no one will look at me like I'm strange. And the good thing is that it's not only a kind of therapy for me, but I can also use it to dispel the fears of other people.'

'I used to want to go into military service to be able to humiliate men and have them march to my tune because, in my opinion, men deserve this – many men deserve this. And then all of a sudden I discovered the job of being a dominatrix and I thought to myself: "Hey, it works much faster this way!"'

'Of course it's also a kind of prostitution. To say "I'm a dominatrix, I'm better than that" is nonsense. It's just different. Prostitutes let someone get closer to them physically; as a dominatrix, you have to let them get closer psychologically. In general, everyone decides for himself what's allowed and what's not. But in my opinion, there's no difference, since it's basically a question of gratification.'

‘Physical contact is very important. This underscores the energy that gets exchanged. Completely unapproachable dominatrices will have a hard time in this business.’

‘I was actually only looking for a completely normal job in the newspaper, because the restaurant where I was working as a waitress had closed down. I’m going to work as a dominatrix for as long as I enjoy it! Men play with model trains and cars; I play with men. It has nothing to do with my sexual preferences.’

‘I’m not selling myself, but rather my services. Whether I serve coffee or spank someone, it’s all the same to me.’

‘I’m still working full-time as a dominatrix, but I’ll soon begin training in the care sector again. I really enjoy working with people. After my training is over, I’d like to work in the field of palliative care. Helping people during difficult phases in their lives has a lot in common with the dominatrix business.’

‘My God! I was born an asshole; I’m not play-acting.’

‘The job can only really work until you become dependent on it. When you realise that something isn’t right, that’s when you have to stop, immediately, but many can’t stop because they need the money.’

‘I started after I began studying medicine. But I had always had such ideas and also went to some fetish clubs. So I already knew quite a bit. Not like many others, who first work as prostitutes and then think it’s easier as a dominatrix, which is not true at all.’

‘What I would like to be asked is: “Do you make your clients happy?” Because no one cares at all about why people go to dominatrices! Instead, most people have a preconceived notion and say: “Oh, sure! He’s perverse; he’s sick. That’s why he has to go there.” And then I always say: “He’s a completely normal person, who walks around with his desires and has no idea where he should go with these. And then, in his desperation, he goes to someone who he doesn’t even know and completely exposes himself, all to be able to live out his desires.” Do I want to make my clients happy? Of course; for me, this is one of the outcomes of my work, to say it was pleasurable, it was enjoyable, it was enjoyable for both of us.’

‘Even if I didn’t make money for doing this, I would still do one guest a day. One hour. I need that for my own gratification.’

‘I can be as cold as ice; that’s the sadistic side of me. And at some point I simply realised that I enjoy doing it. I enjoy it when people are afraid of me.’

‘A good dominatrix is not egoistic; I truly believe that. You have to be empathetic, you have to be open and ready to perceive and experience the person across from you.’

‘You should only take what you can handle, especially in this field. It’s wrong to come out of a session and feel disgusted, to shake it off and then buy something with the money you just earned, only to feel a sense of happiness again.’

‘The stars were always able to do such things, Lady Gaga and company in leather, latex and rubber, even bondage.’

‘First and foremost, I’m a completely normal woman. This existence as a dominatrix is not my life.’

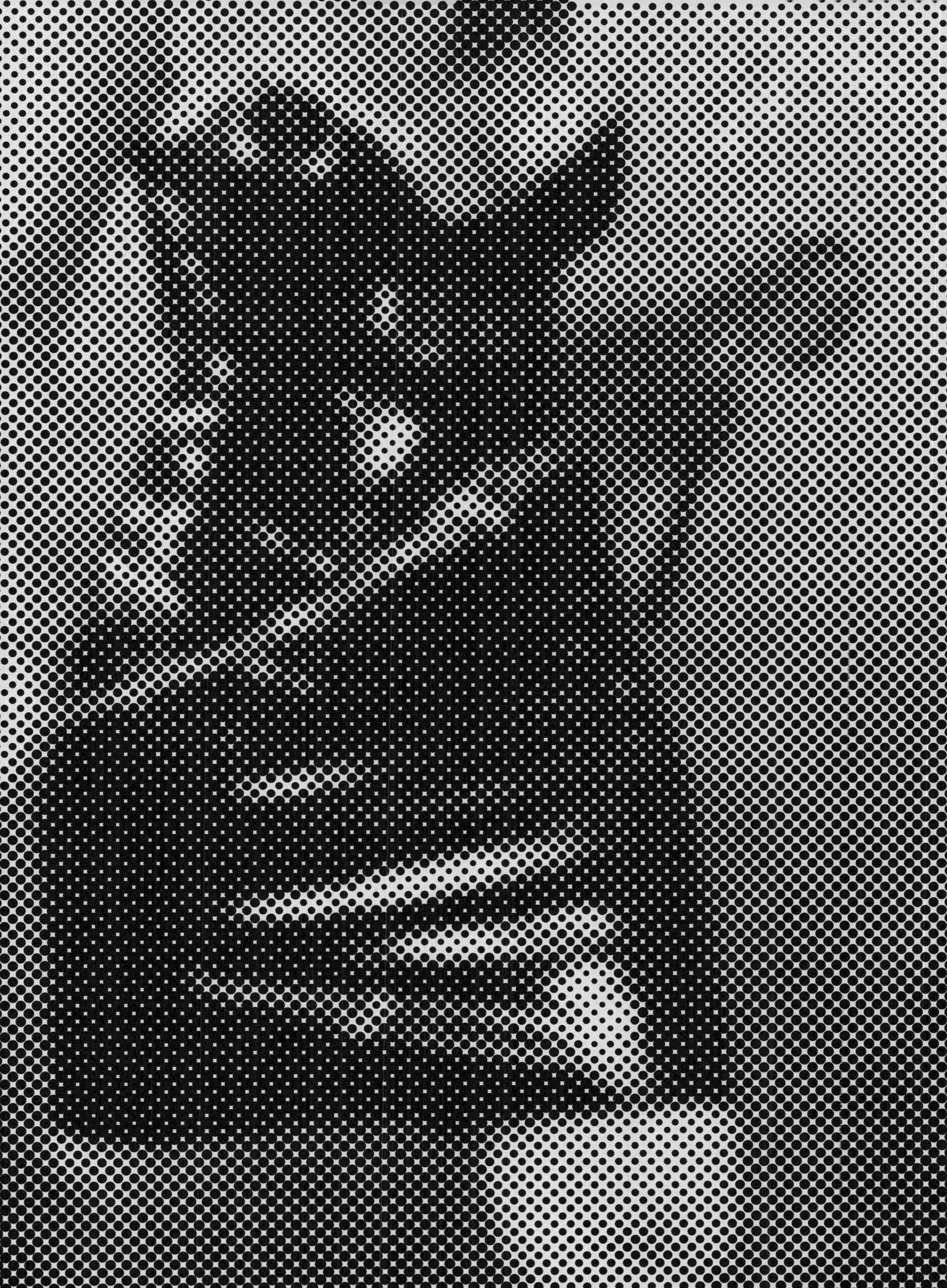

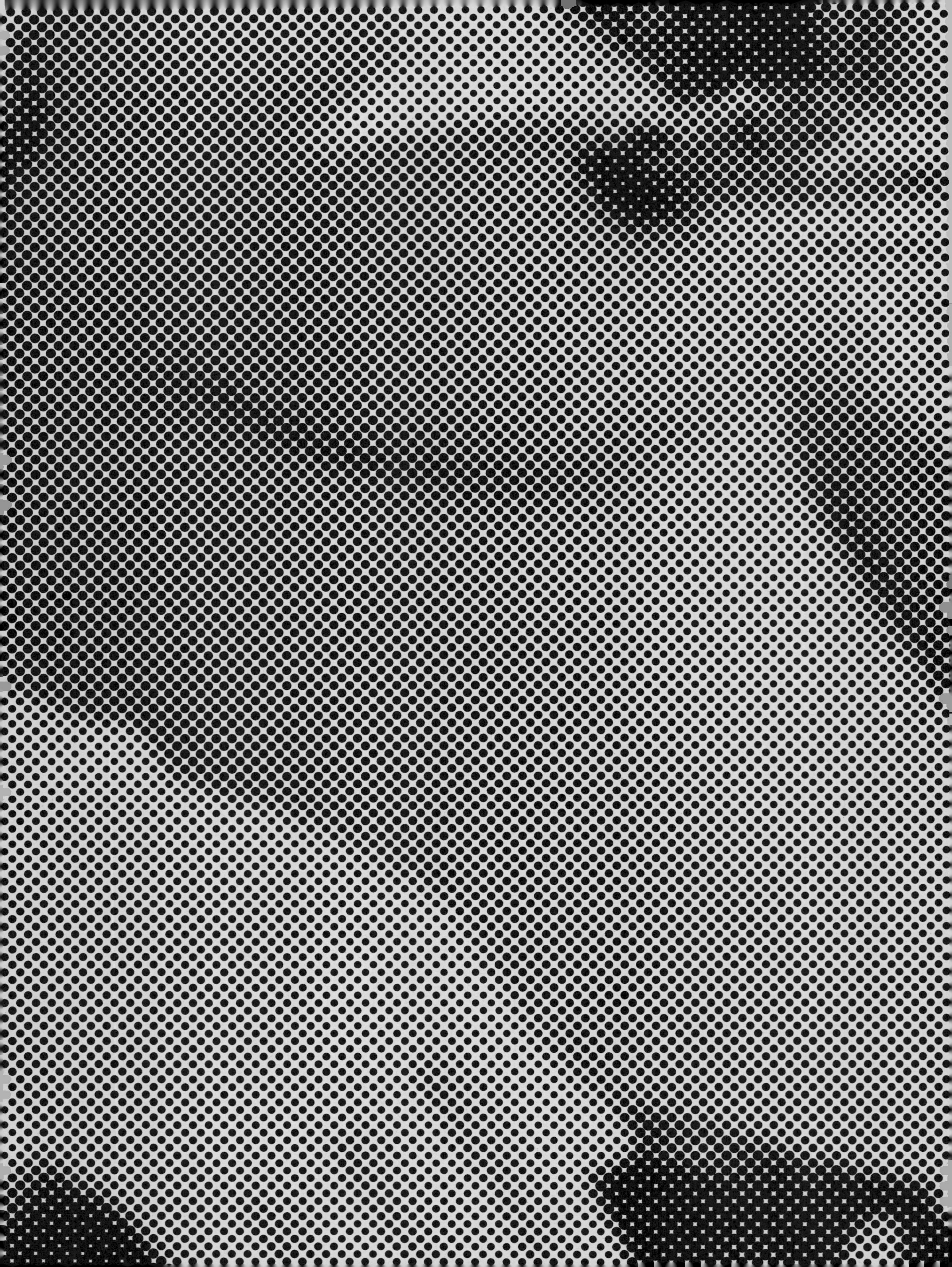

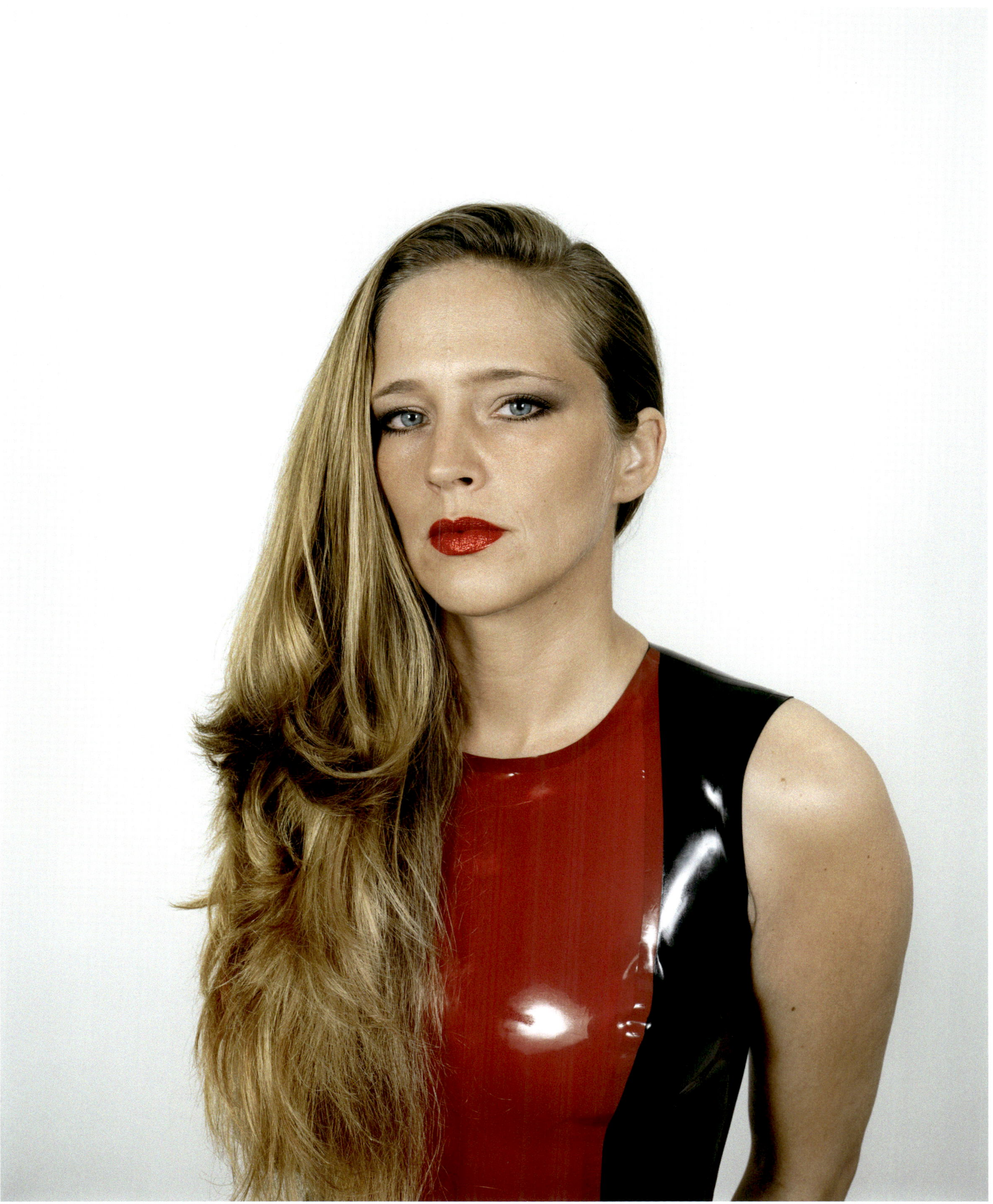

DIVINE YAMUNA · Munich, 2014

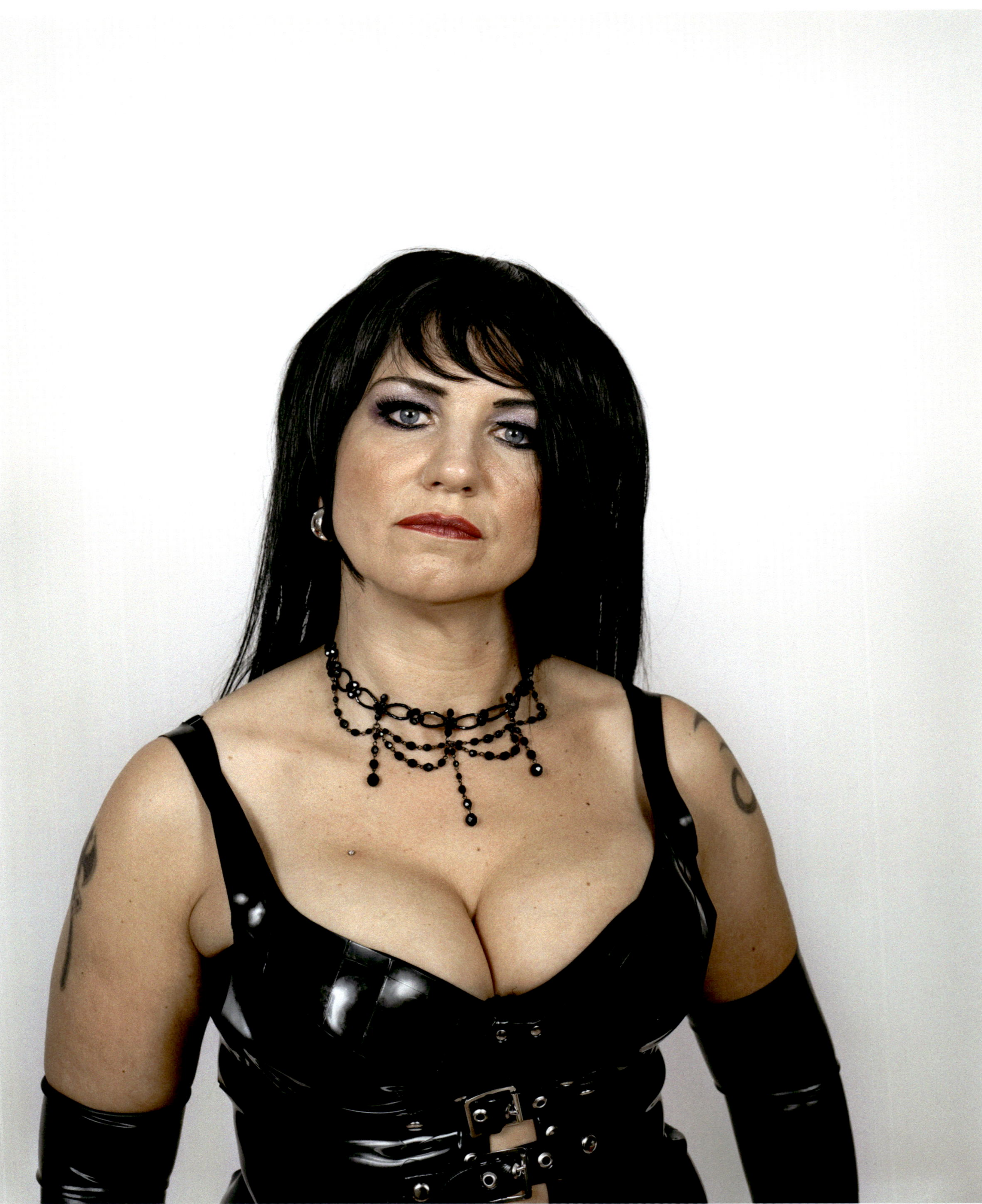

LADY SUSANNA · Munich, 2013

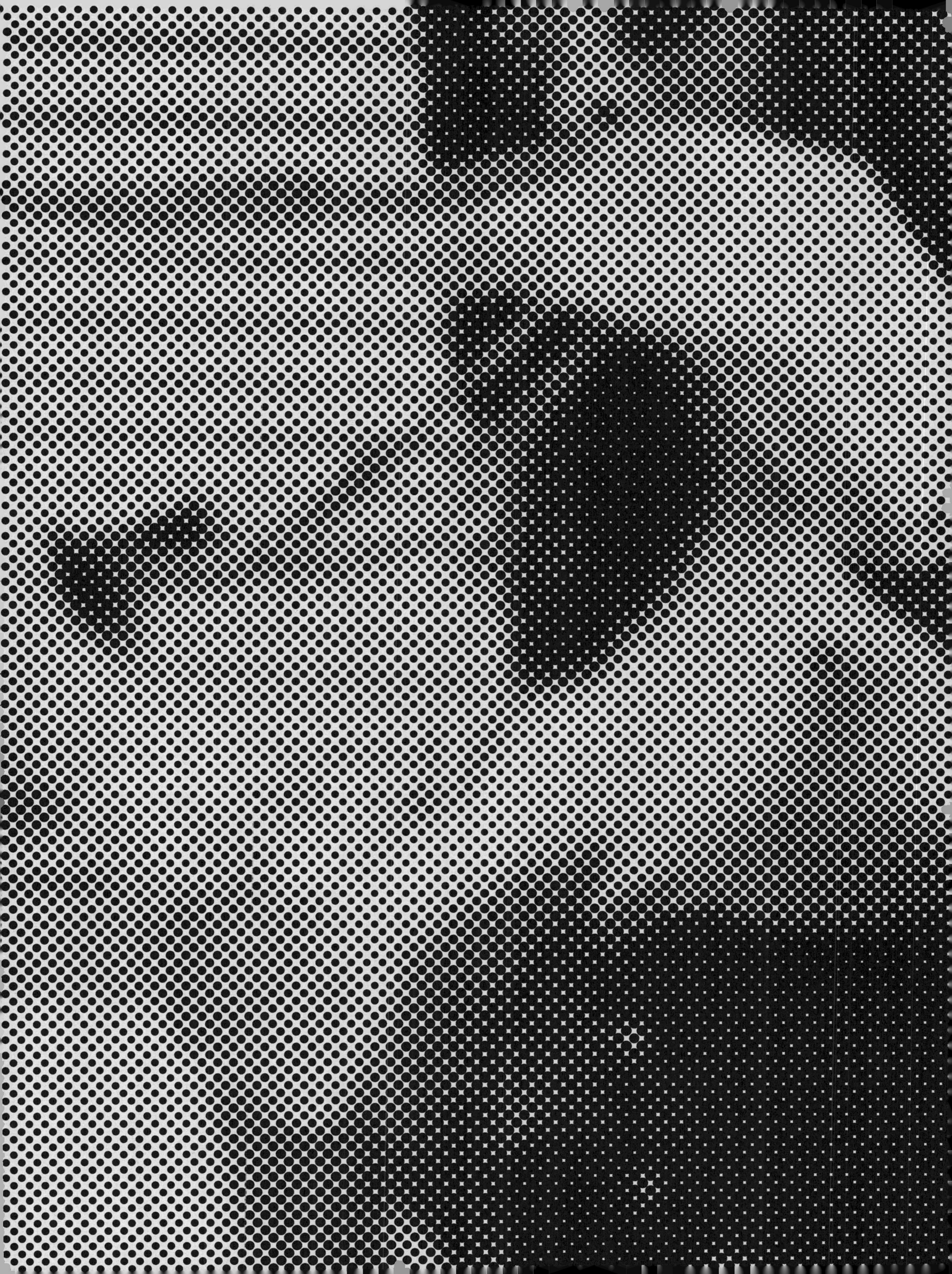

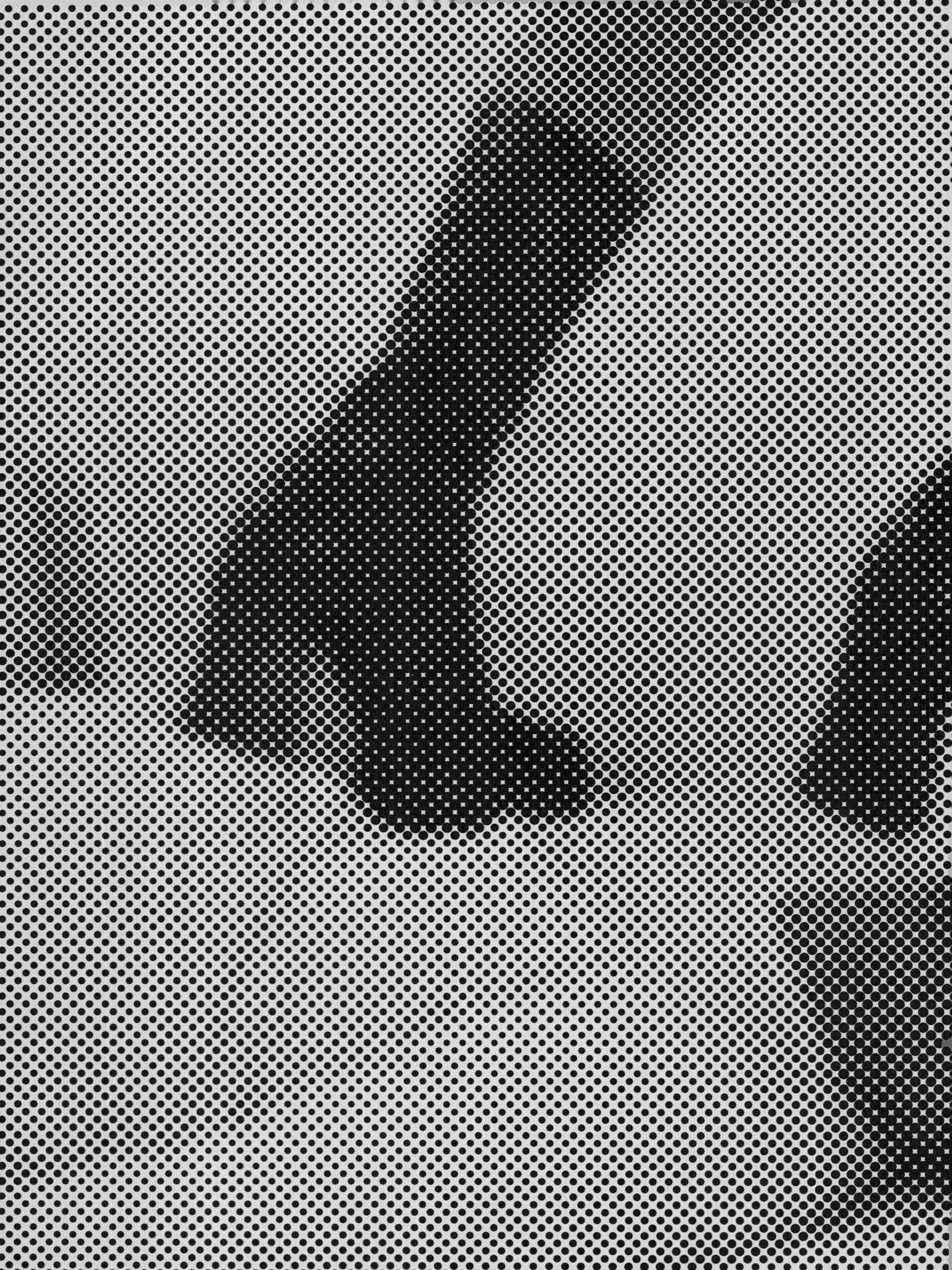

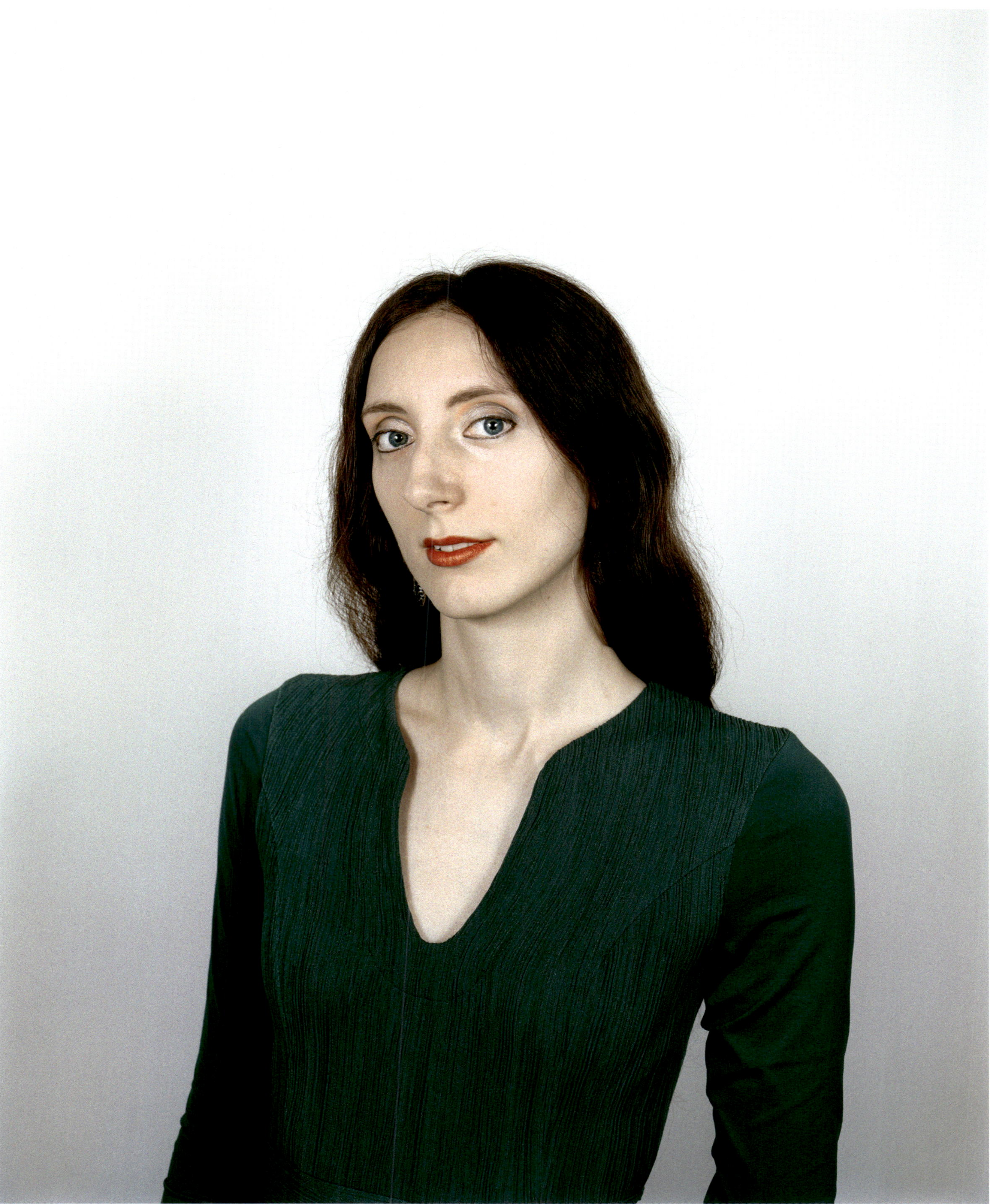

MADEMOISELLE LOUISE · Berlin, 2014

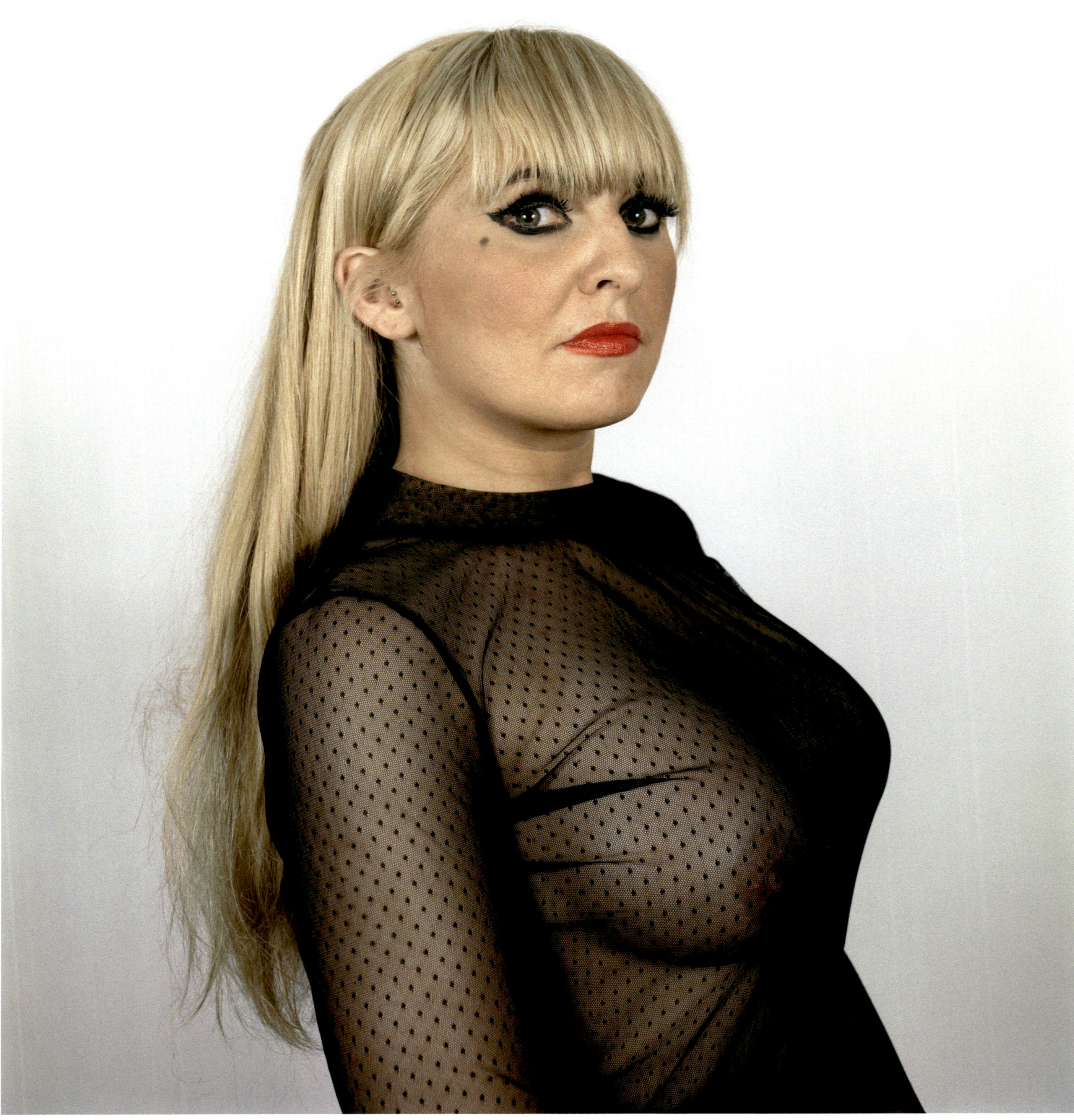

LADY ELECTRA · Munich, 2015

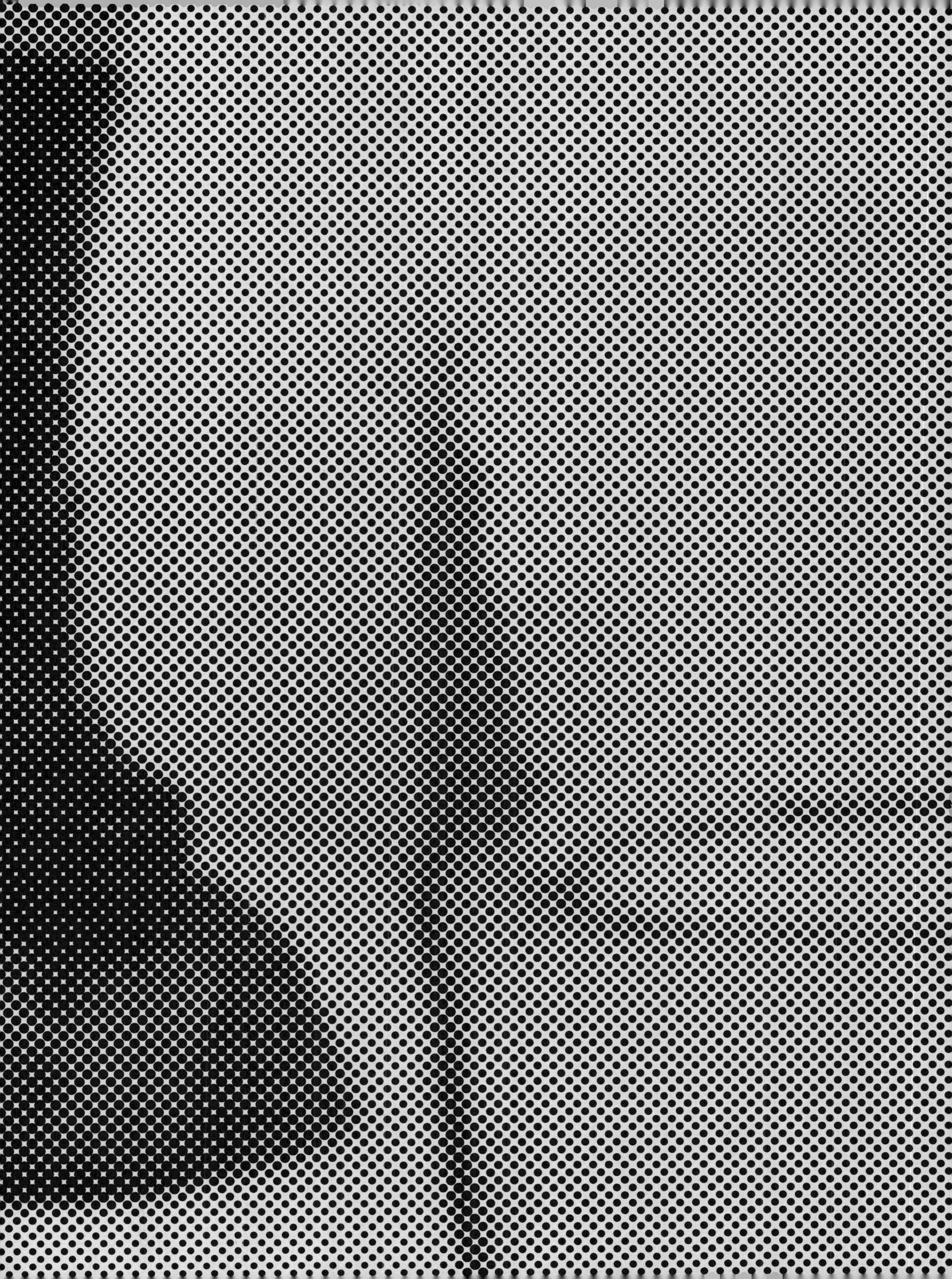

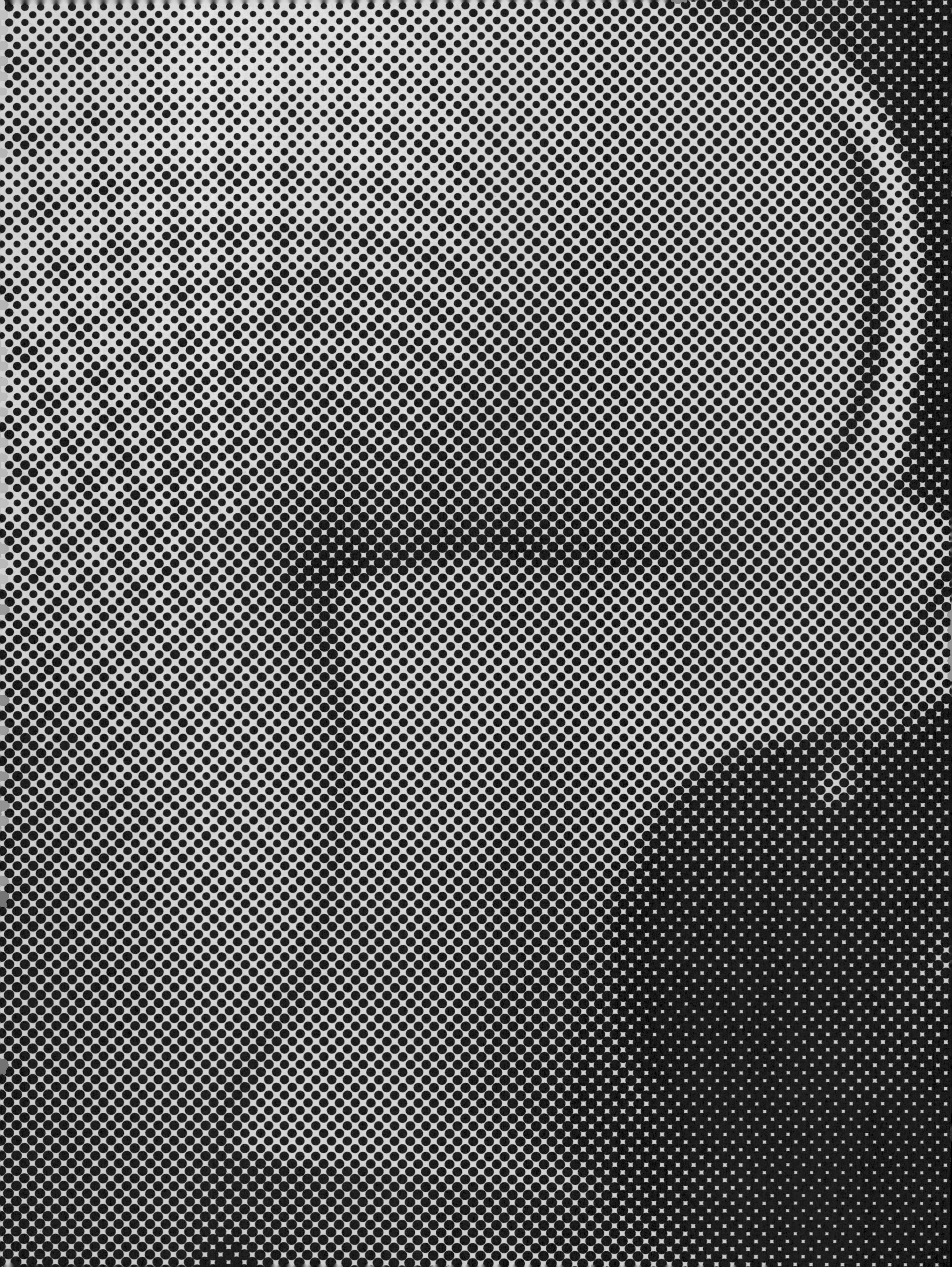

‘When a grown man lies there in front of you crying because he’s so grateful and happy, that’s very impressive.’

‘Guests trust me 100 percent. I get told stories no one else even knows, in some cases not even their best friends. No one, no one, no one. And that’s exactly the point about honesty: You’re honest with yourself and that’s the beginning – not being honest with other people, but rather dealing with yourself in an honest way.’

‘I’ve also had politicians and celebrities. Basically, I don’t really care what they do – they can even be construction workers – but it has to fit. The Swiss are very demanding, Austrians are very demanding, people from Munich are very demanding.’

‘The fact that someone enjoys pain is a kind of predisposition; not everyone has this in them, of course. But to enjoy handing over control sometimes, or taking control – I think everyone has this in them. I also think that almost everyone has both sides in them – a dominant side and a submissive side.’

‘Dominance is hard work. I have no desire to take on responsibility for someone on a permanent basis. It’s a game. In a game, it’s fun to take someone to his limits. Everyone has different ideas. I don’t inflict pain upon anyone who doesn’t ask for it beforehand.’

'You can't be a slave one day and a king the next – that doesn't work. But you also can't simply become a king – that also doesn't work. You have to be made for both.'

'I also don't treat my guests like a piece of dirt. I treat them poorly – but poorly with respect.'

'I find it sad that many women who have nothing to do with it in their private lives see it from a purely commercial perspective and also have a very unfair opinion of their clients. On the one hand, they gratify their clients, and on the other hand they say: "They're all just sick and perverse" and "just imagine that you had a husband and he was the same way – that would be disgusting."'

'Making people dependent – for me, this is power, and it turns me on.'

'Being dominant does not mean forcing someone to do something. Being dominant means making someone want you to force him.'

'For me, respect for the guest is extremely important. For me, he's not a punter; for me, he's a human being. I find it important to recognise the wishes and desires of every individual and to say to them: "It's perfectly fine the way it is!"'

‘When I know that he’s in great pain, but endures it for my sake – this makes me proud as a dominatrix. After the pain comes the reward, even when it’s only a hand that caresses his face.’

‘Sadism and power are very strong emotions, which release certain hormones. As a dominatrix, I live out my sadistic desires more than my sexual ones. Sexuality paired with sadism and power is something I only live out in private with my partner. But I find power within a game of S&M to be extremely sexy. It’s a good feeling to have control over someone. But I find the exercising of power in “real life” to be completely senseless. We should all be equal.’

‘I enjoy the game of closeness and distance because I enjoy tension. The more tension there is, the more exciting it is. And in this job, less is simply more. If I were to sleep with a guest and let him feel me up, the game would be too easy.’

‘When I see a twinkle in his eye, when I get a reaction – that’s when I have fun. This is important for me. If it was only about making the man happy, I’d go crazy.’

‘I find it important to maintain a sense of humour and humanity, to not take it all too seriously and to never forget: I’m a human, he’s a human; and it’s exciting for both of us.’

‘It’s a topsy-turvy world anyway; I mean, if they were really slaves, I would never have asked them what they like, what they don’t like – I wouldn’t give a shit. Why do we have a wish list and taboos? It’s actually the other way around – the mistress fulfils the wishes of her slaves.’

‘Once, after a session, I went with one of my clients for a stroll in the park. For two hours, we talked almost exclusively about sex. I had to pull myself together the whole time so as not to fall all over him, because I thought he was extremely hot. After the stroll, I had to find out; I just couldn’t let him walk away… And he was an extremely good kisser. Yeah, you can never say that it can’t happen to you too.’

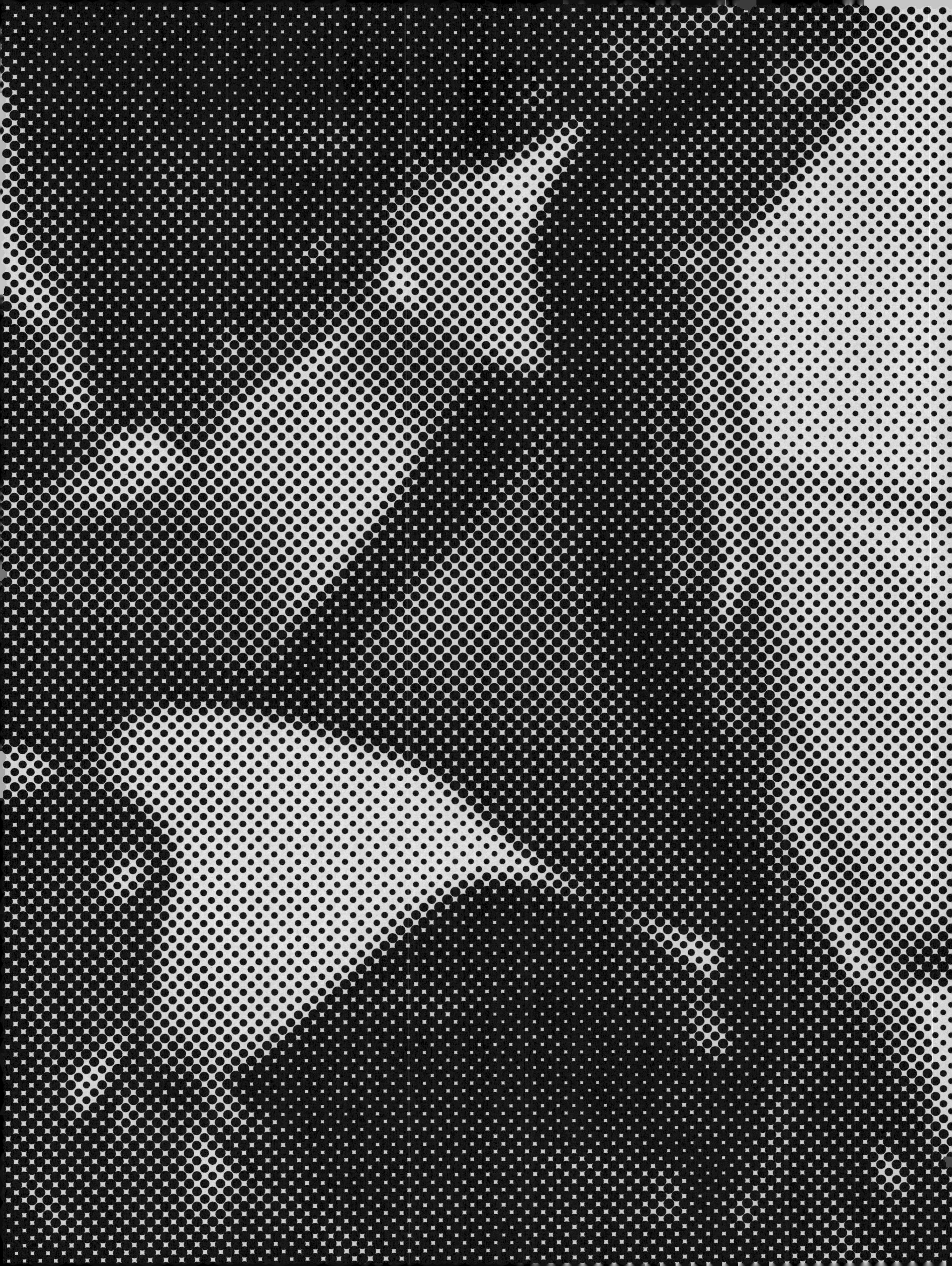

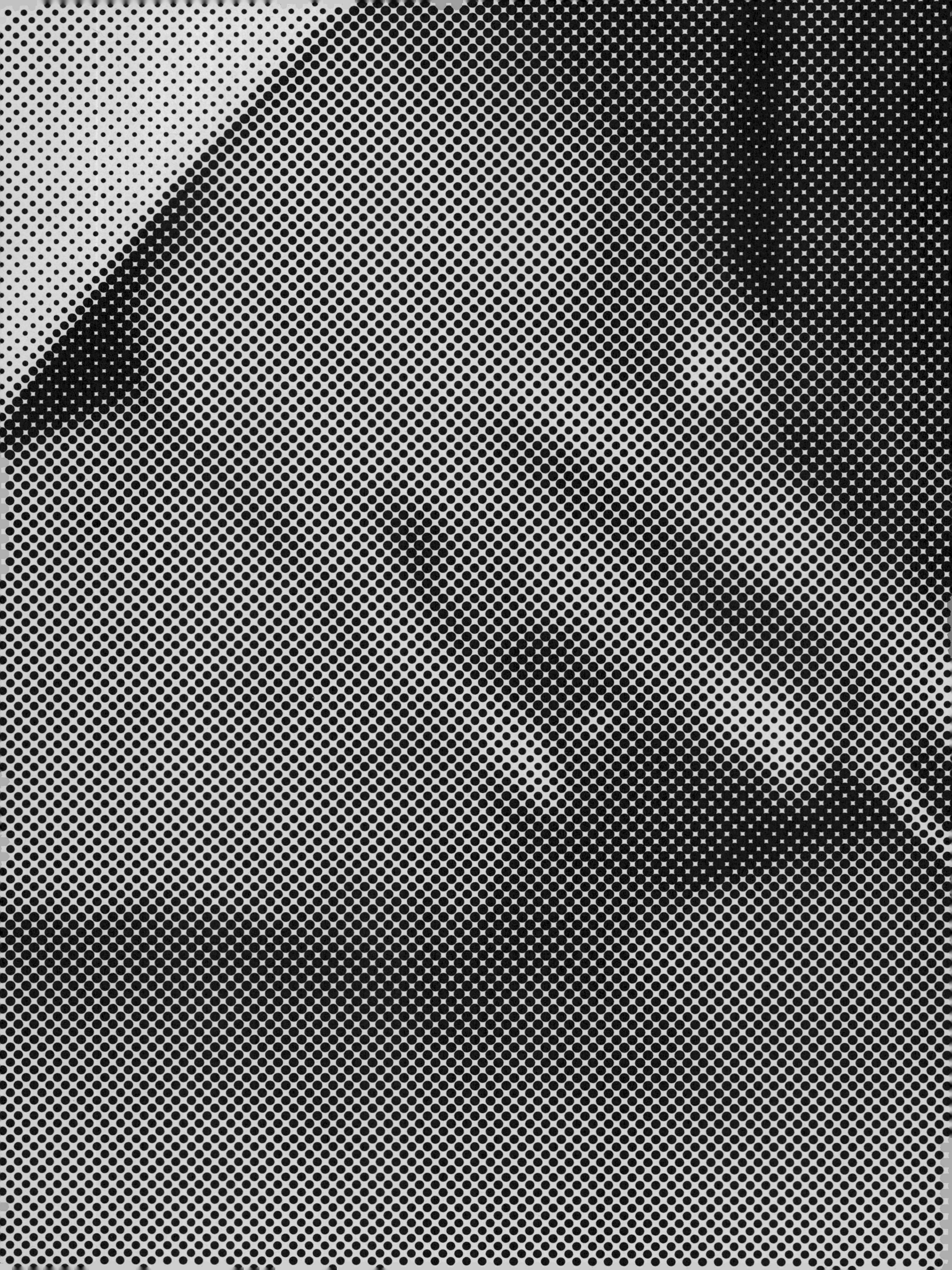

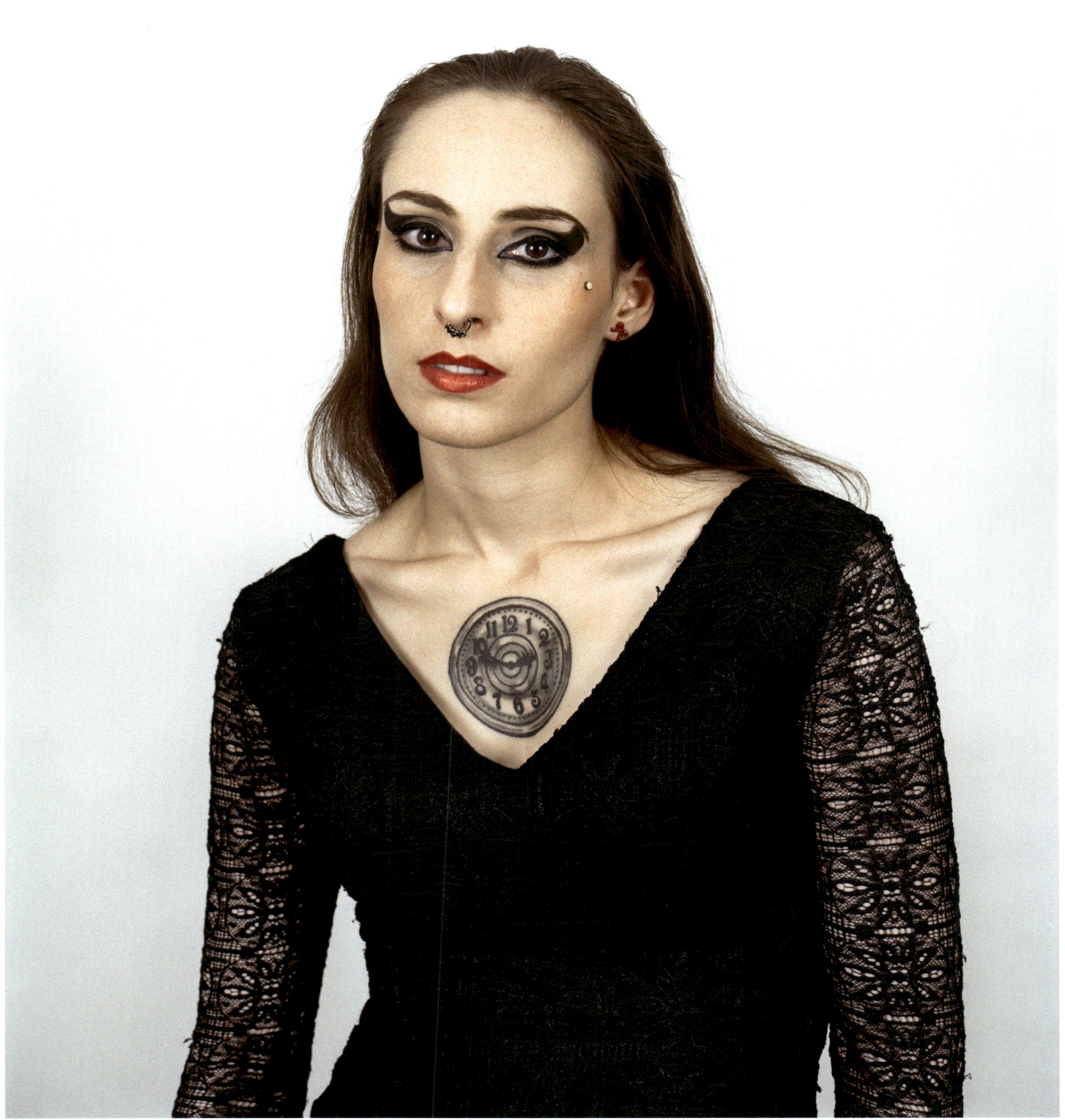

LADY ROXANNE · Stuttgart, 2016

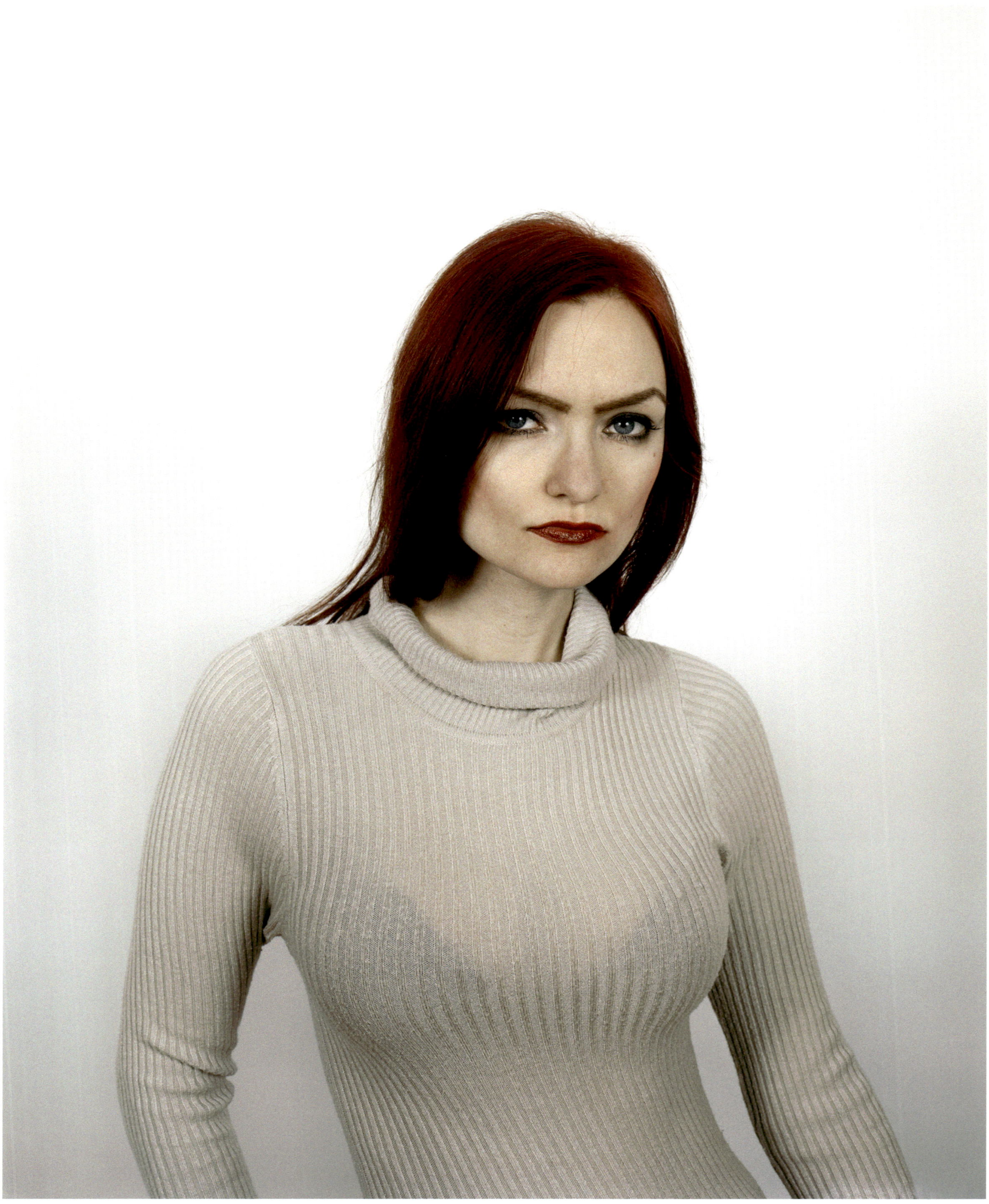

FRÄULEIN SCHMIDT · Munich, 2014

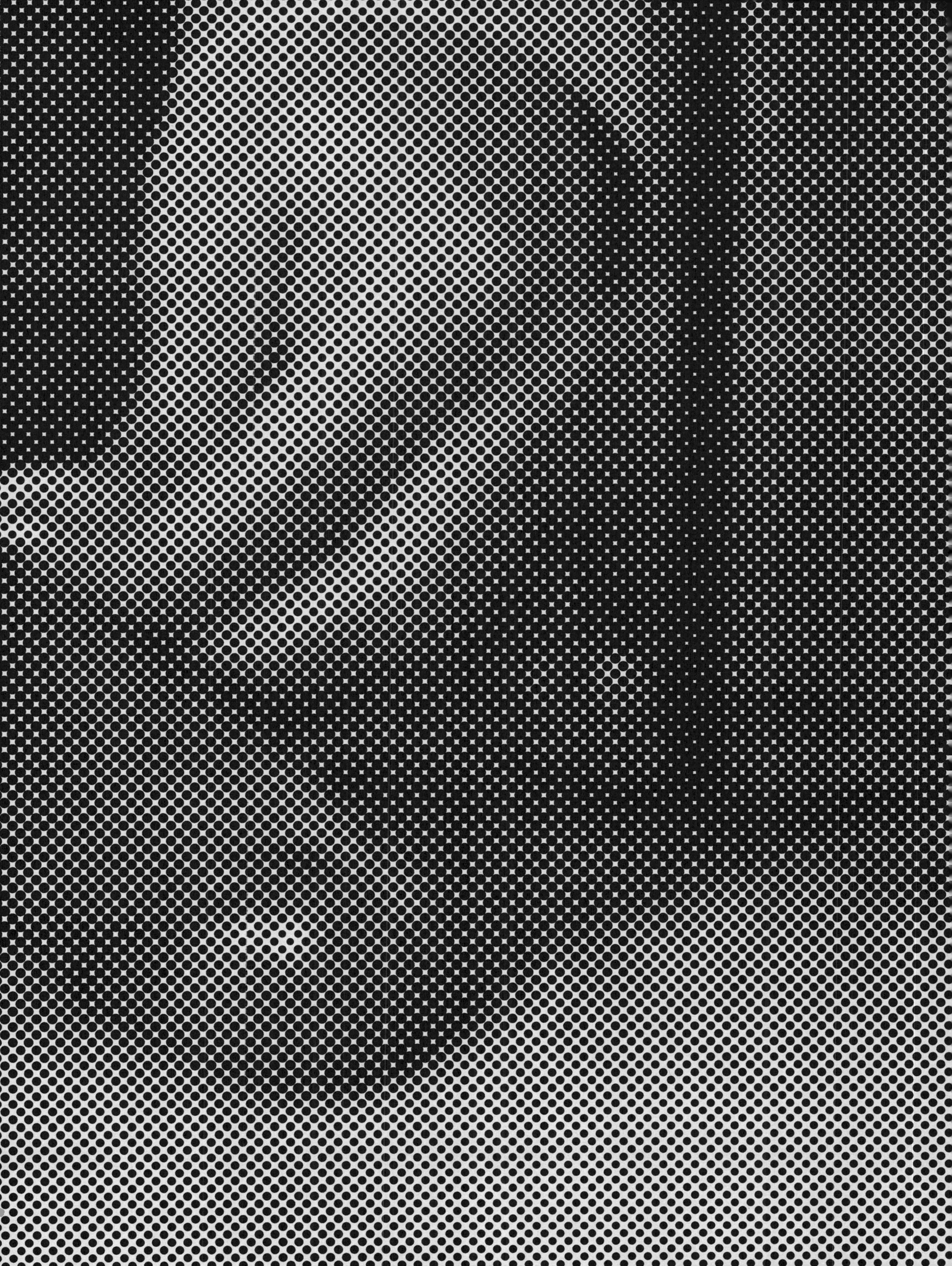

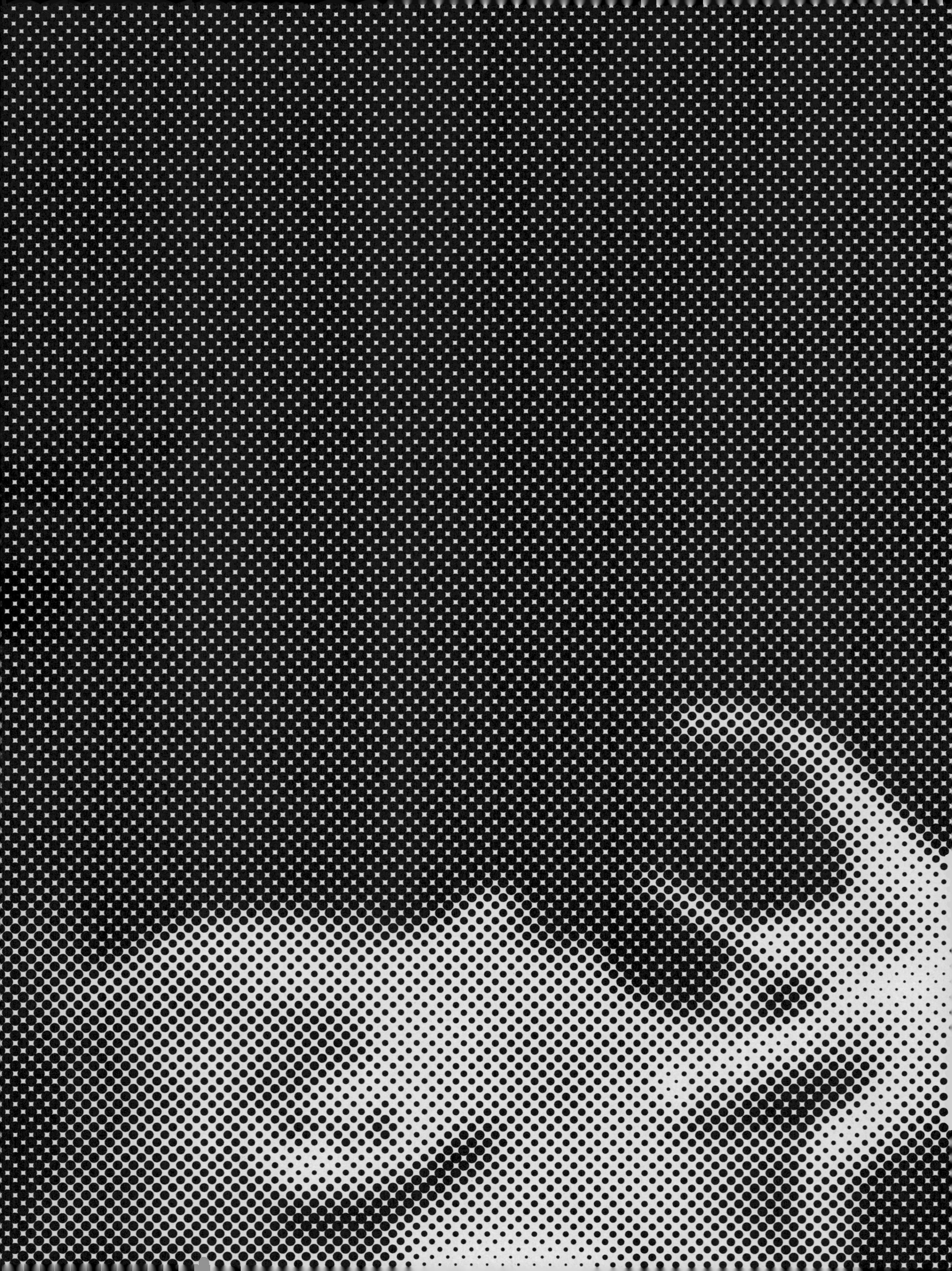

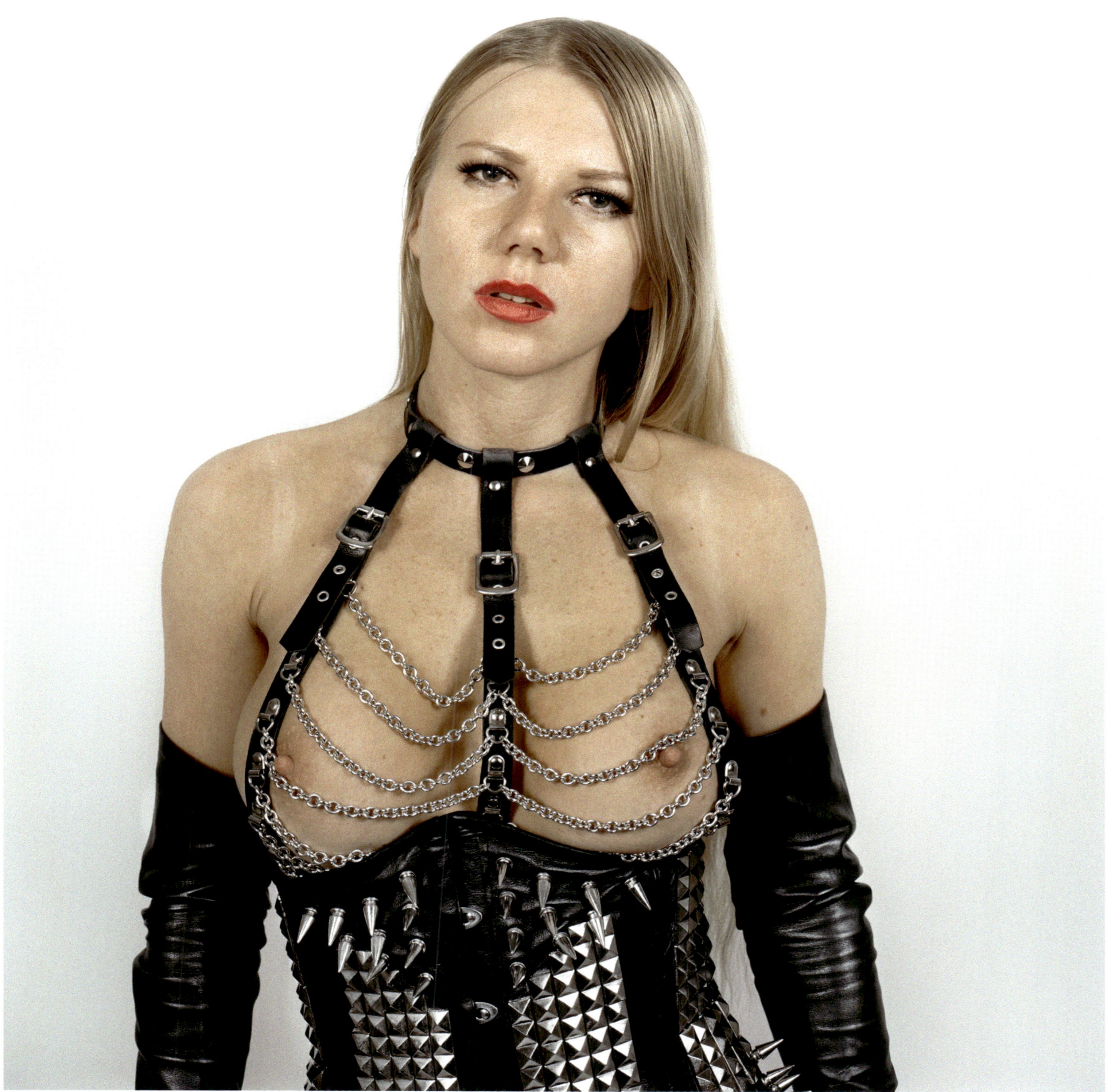

BIZARRLADY ESTELLE · Cologne, 2015

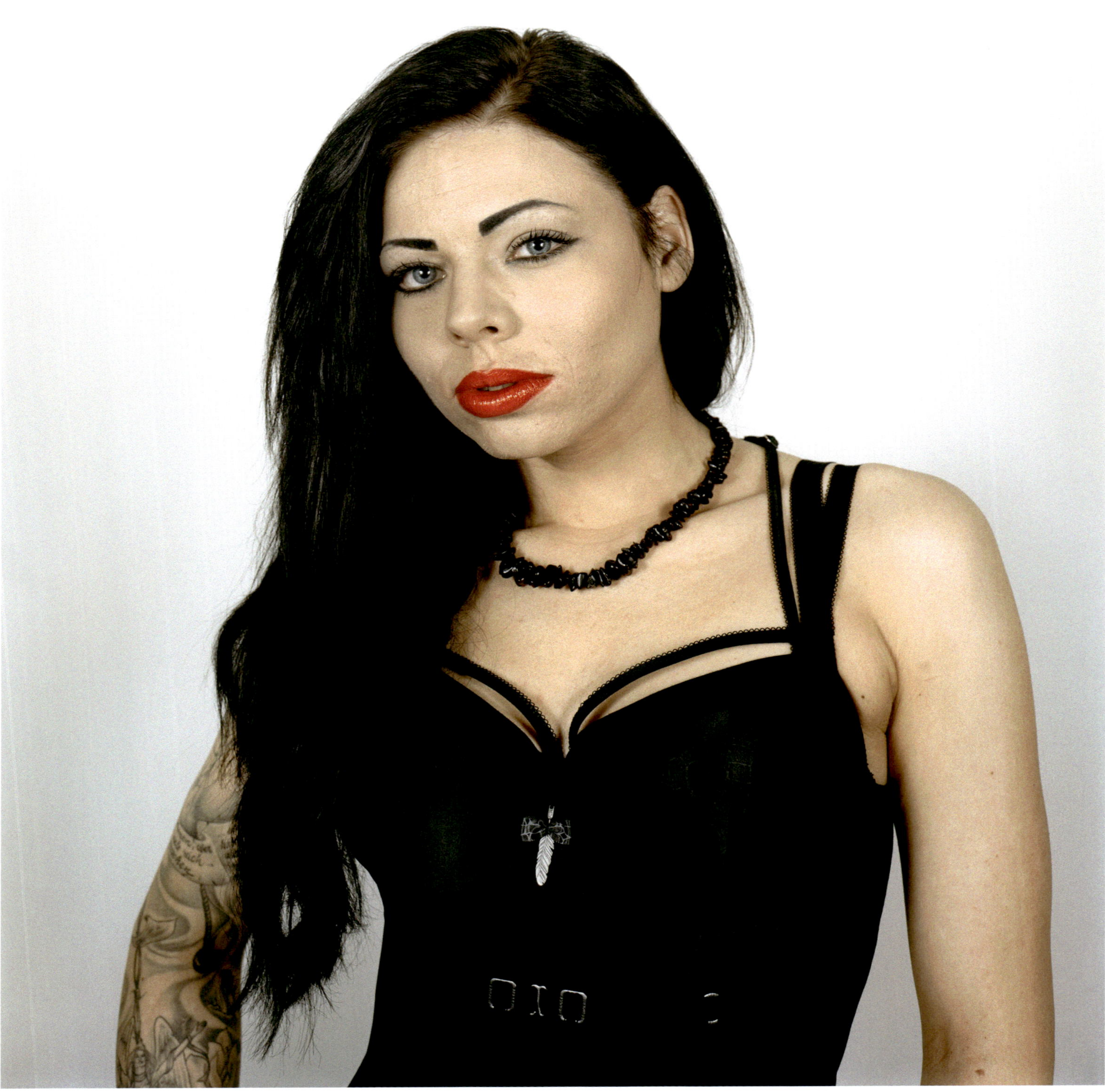

LADY ASHLEY · Leipzig, 2014

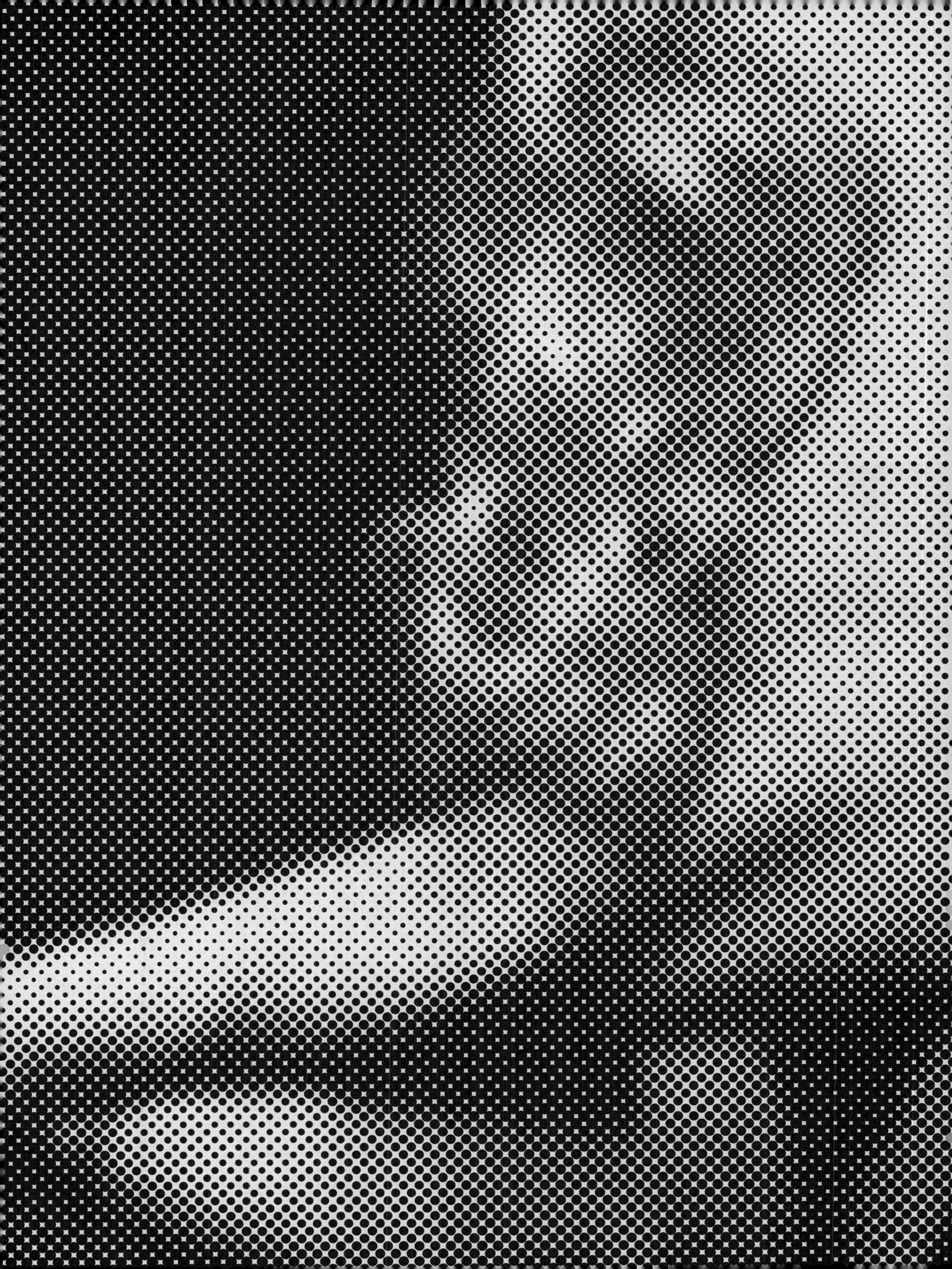

'I don't fit the bill of a dominatrix, which is actually quite good.'

'It's not always pleasant to be immediately confronted with rejection as soon as you tell someone what you do, when you're dealing with someone who only thinks in terms of stereotypes. All of sudden, everything else that contributes to who you are can be thrown into the dustbin, because it's no longer interesting, doesn't count at all anymore, is not even worth mentioning, simply because you're a dominatrix. But it's also not my job to enlighten them; I'm not a missionary or any of that rubbish. I'm simply me.
I don't have to make everyone like me.'

'So at some point I told my mother and all she could say was: "Well, as long as they don't take it out on small children." What kind of idea is that? Just because someone goes to an S&M studio doesn't mean that he's a child molester. Too many things that have nothing to do with each other are simply being thrown into the same pot. These are people who have other fantasies than simply "in and out"; they're not perverse men who rape small children.'

'The first thing the men ask when they hear that you're a dominatrix is: "Do you act the same way in your private sex life?" These are the most annoying questions.'

‘I also thought that maybe I could say something like this: Yes, I worked as a dominatrix; I even made a porn film. Look at me! I’m not dumb; I studied medicine, and even did a second degree. And I did it because I wanted to. I didn’t have a ponce, and I made a deliberate decision to do it. Why don’t you even want to take a closer look?’

‘You also have to learn how to use a whip.’

‘So many women work in this field because of a lack of alternatives.’

‘I’ve also had problems with studio owners and colleagues, simply because I’ve said time and again: “I don’t want that” or “I won’t do that”. You cannot become dependent, neither on money nor on the people you work for or your clients. You have to remain independent, and even if you are dependent, we live here in a country where no one has to go hungry. There are enough jobs and, if worst comes to worst, the state will even come to the rescue. You don’t have to sell your soul in order to eat.’

‘There’s not a whip out there that I don’t know how it feels.’

‘You have to have a certain level of education, otherwise you cannot understand the facets of the human psyche and are thus not qualified for this job.’

‘We do not only consist of sexual activity, of a longing, a desire. In each and every one of us, so much more is going on.’

‘When I realise that my counterpart can truly let loose and let himself go, it’s like a switch has been flipped inside of me; then I’m fully there. I don’t watch the clock, I lose track of space and time, I no longer hear the music playing in the background – then I’m completely and utterly one with the situation. And when, afterwards, I see that he’s smiling, that he’s happy, it brings a smile to my own face and I know that I did everything right, that there’s nothing reprehensible about it.’

‘You don’t have to understand it; there’s no need to comprehend it, you don’t have to participate. And you don’t have to live it, but you also can’t pass judgment and say that it’s wrong. When the guest feels right about it, when he gets a sense of fulfilment from it, when it’s good for him, then it’s fine for him. And when the woman who performs it says she can do it and it takes place without compulsion, then I don’t see anything perverse in it.’

‘For me, perverse is everything that does not take place by mutual consent. To demand something from someone which he doesn’t like and only does out of a sense of courtesy – yeah, when something takes place without consent, then we can talk about perversion.’

‘I believe that if all people were sexually balanced and happy, the world would be a better place. It’s often those who shout the loudest “Hey, it’s perverse!” who have God only knows what kind of fantasies but are ashamed of themselves because they think it’s perverse and pass judgement on themselves, on the inside, and basically think of themselves as a bad person.’

‘Normal is what every person decides it is for themselves. Not what society prescribes for them.’

‘There are certainly relationships in which both say, full of conviction: “I’m faithful.” Out of respect for yourself, respect for your partner; because you’re happy, because you’re content. But when one of you misses something and gets it somewhere else, without questioning the relationship and the emotions, then it’s much better when you’re allowed to do this without having to lie or betray and be a bad person. It’s so much better when it’s simply a relationship based on trust and both say: “Hey, go on, live out your sexual fantasy, and when you come home, I’ll make you a cup of tea.”’

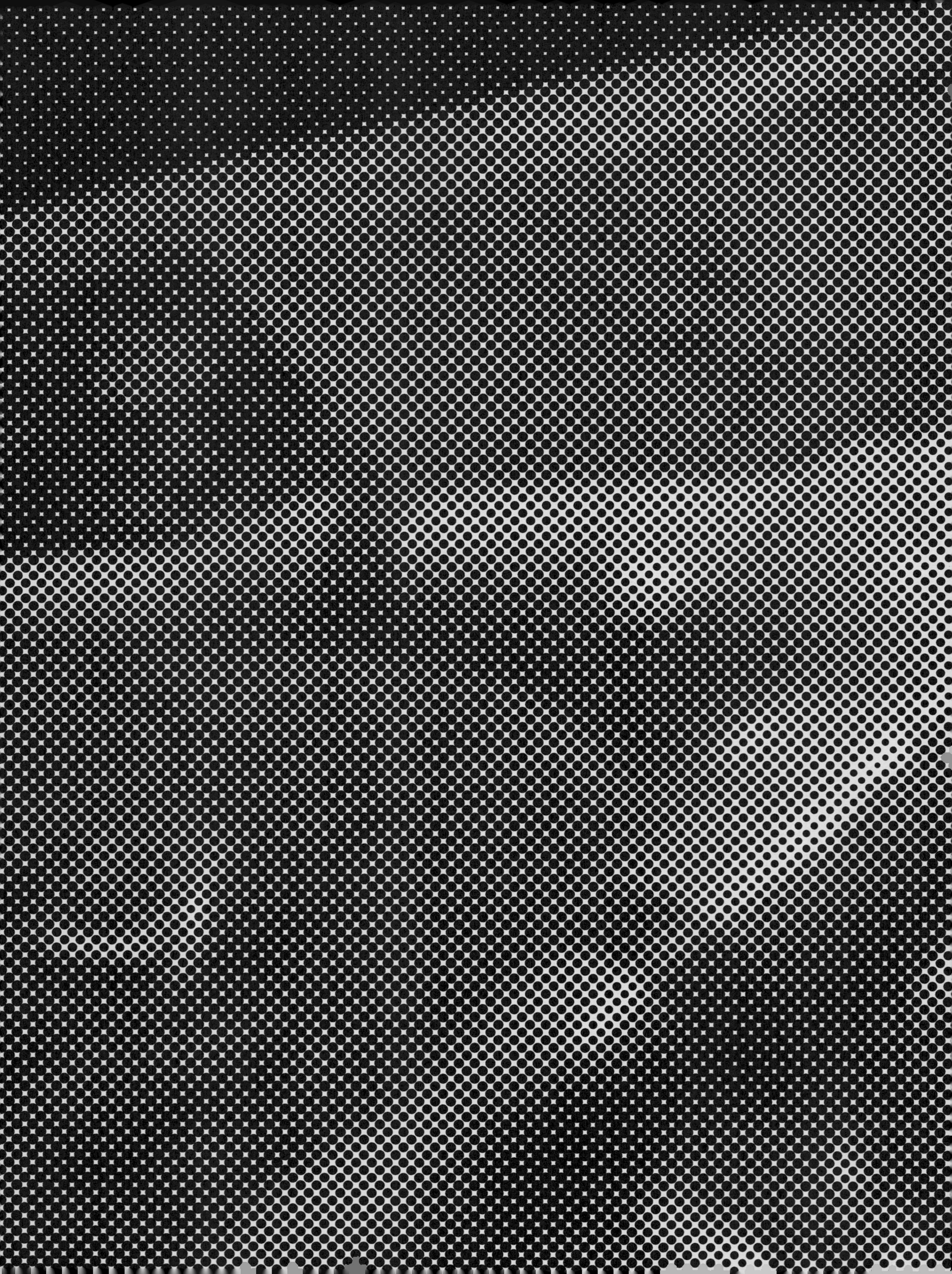

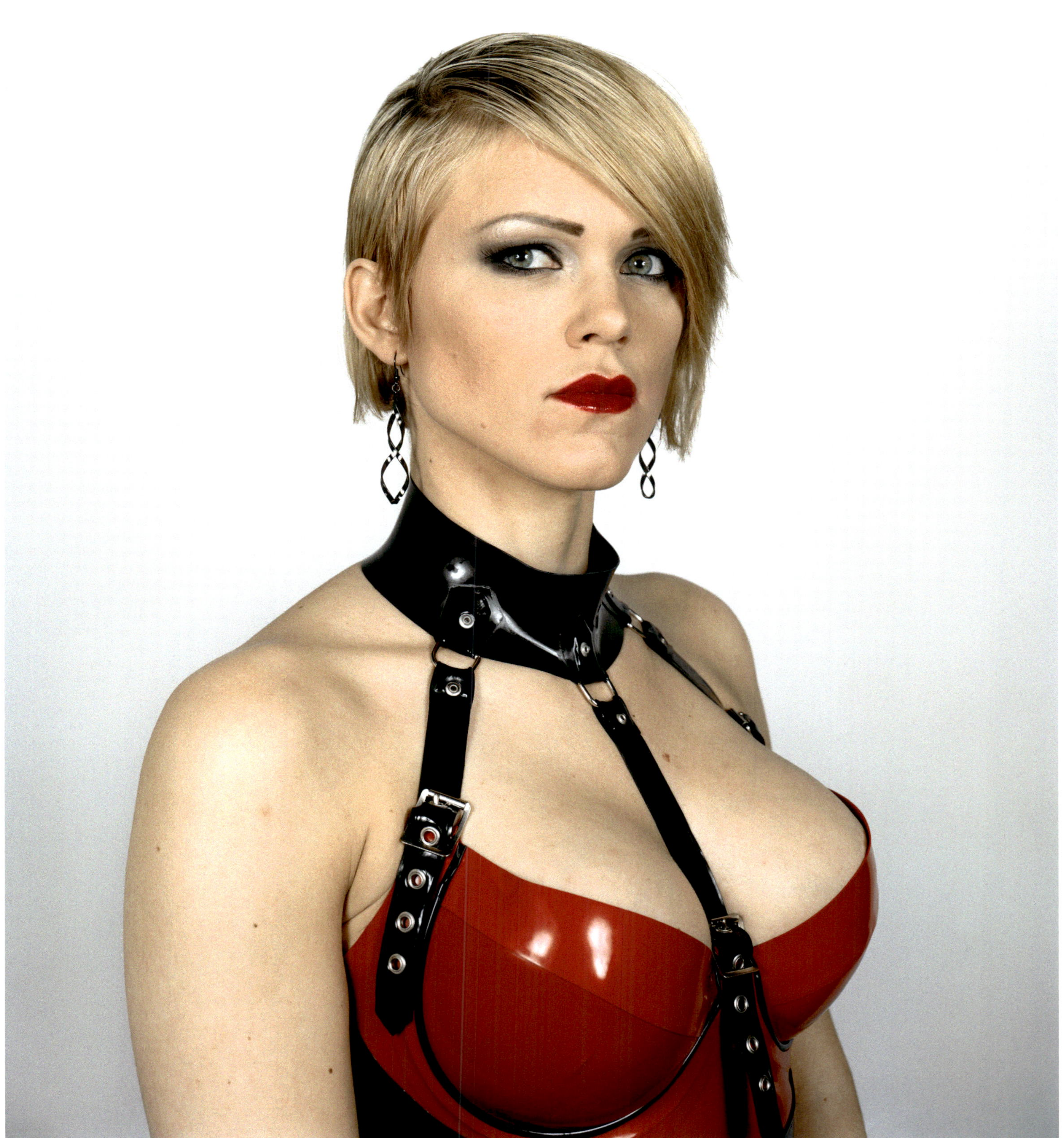

BARONESS DAVINA DUST · Munich, 2013

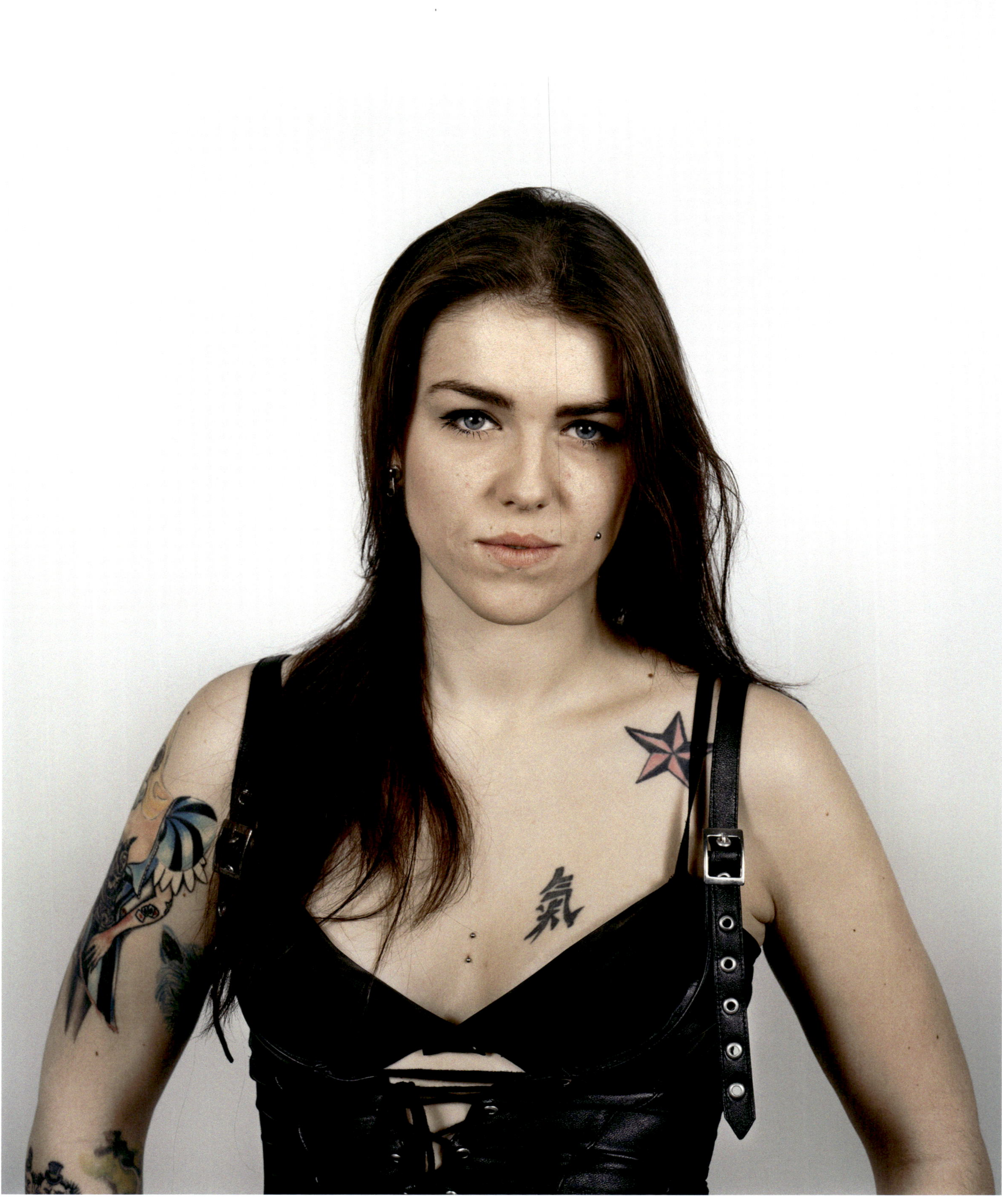

BIZARRLADY VICKY · Berlin, 2014

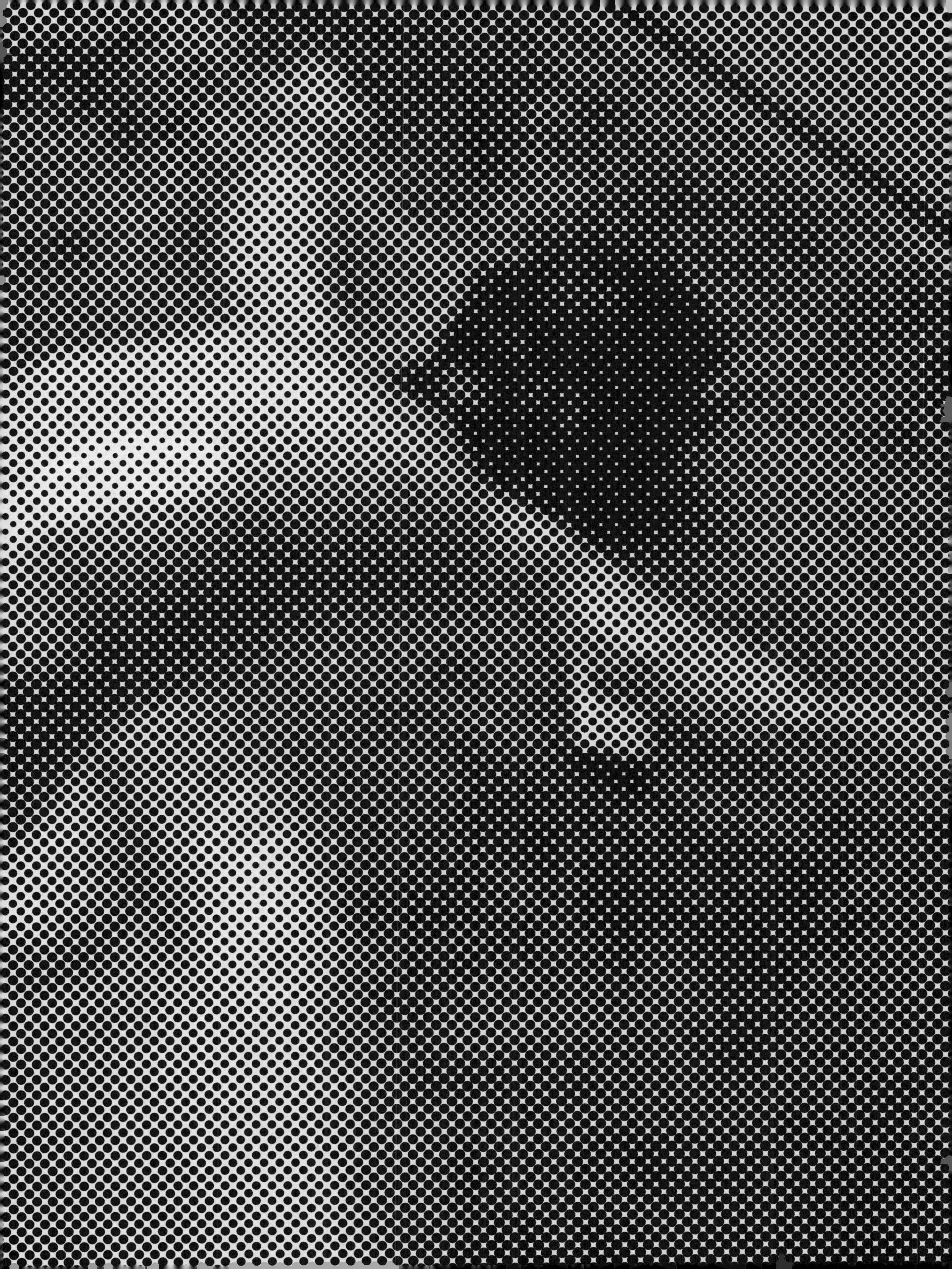

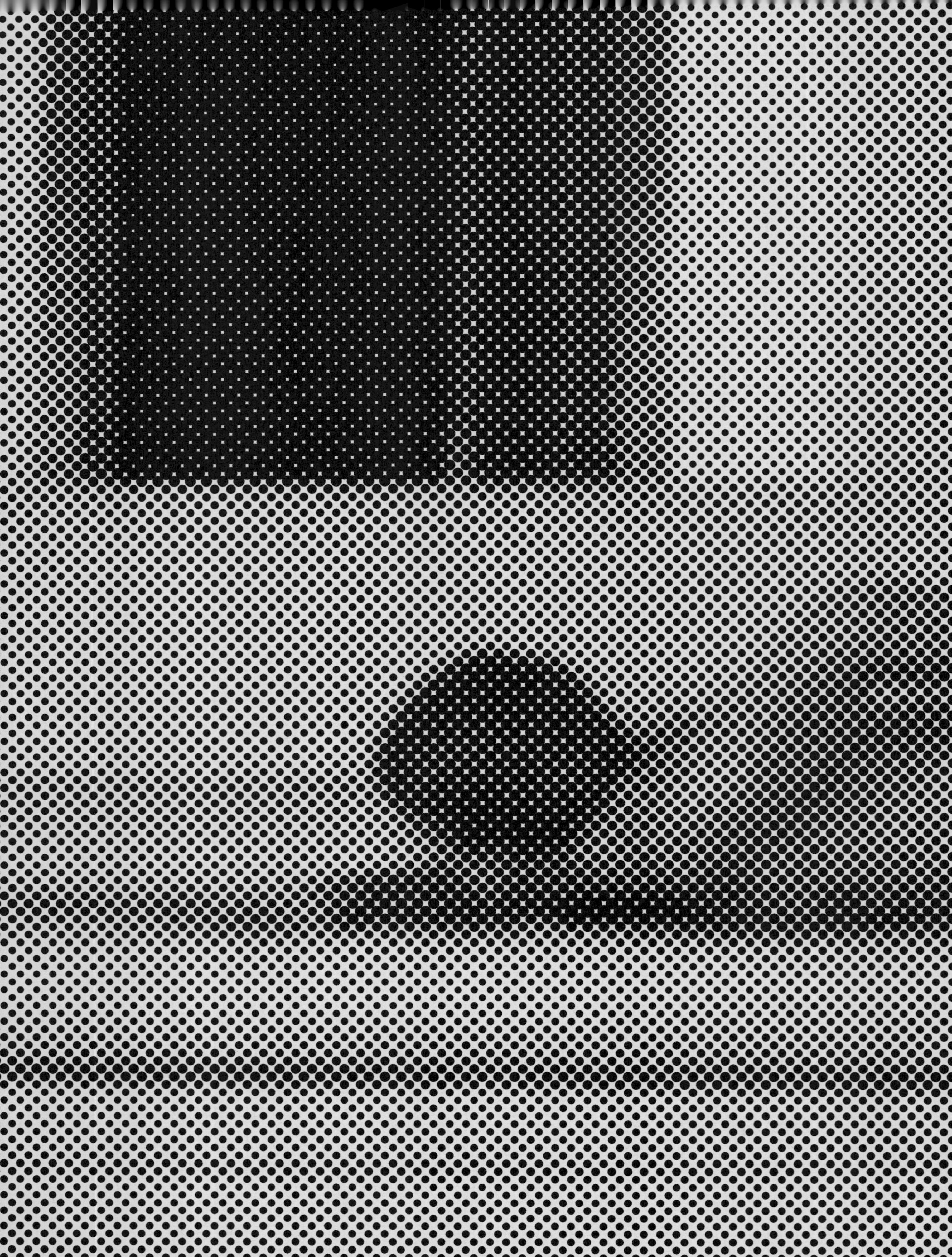

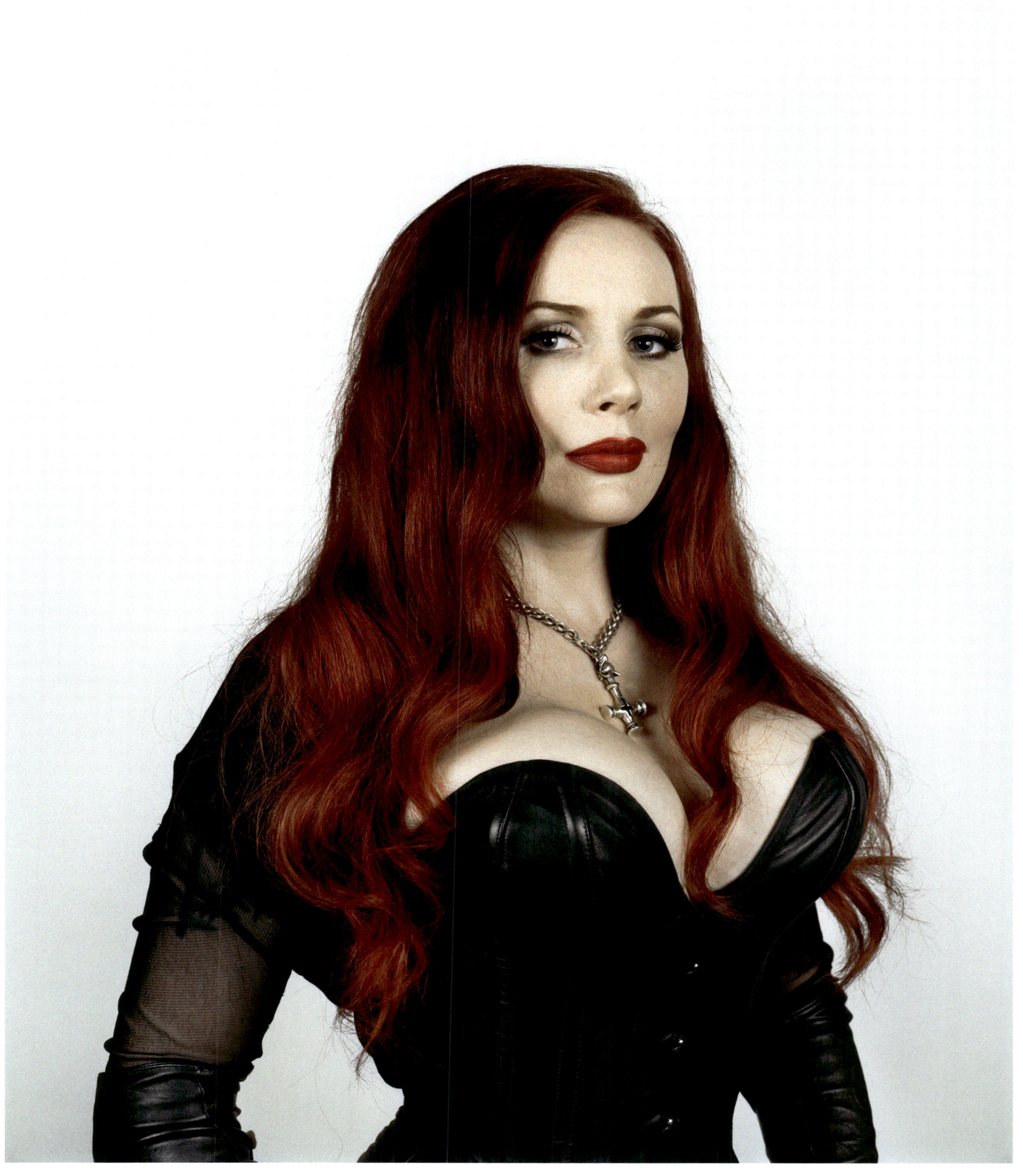

MISTRESS MORRIGAN HEL · London, 2016

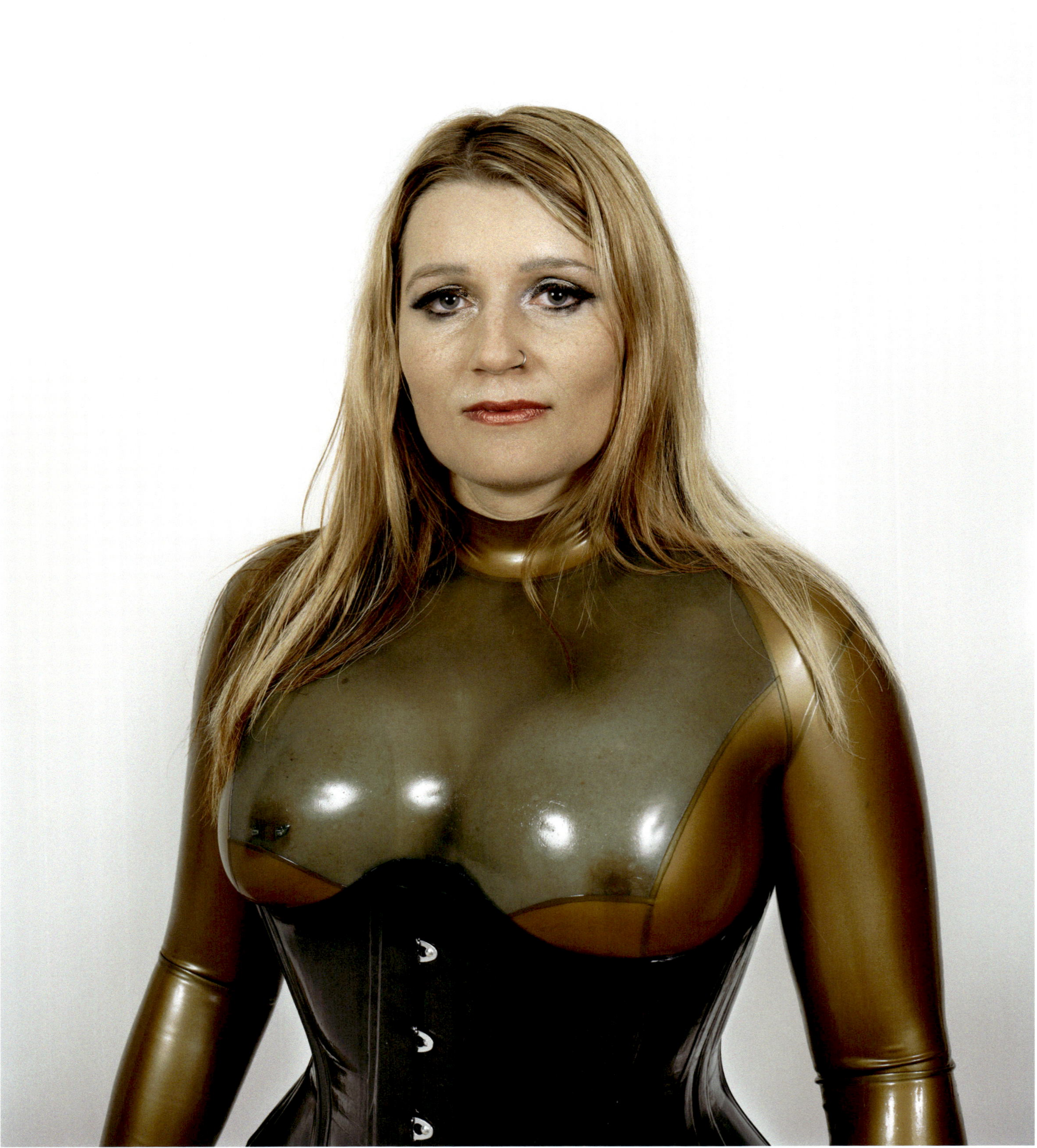

UMA MASOME · Munich, 2014

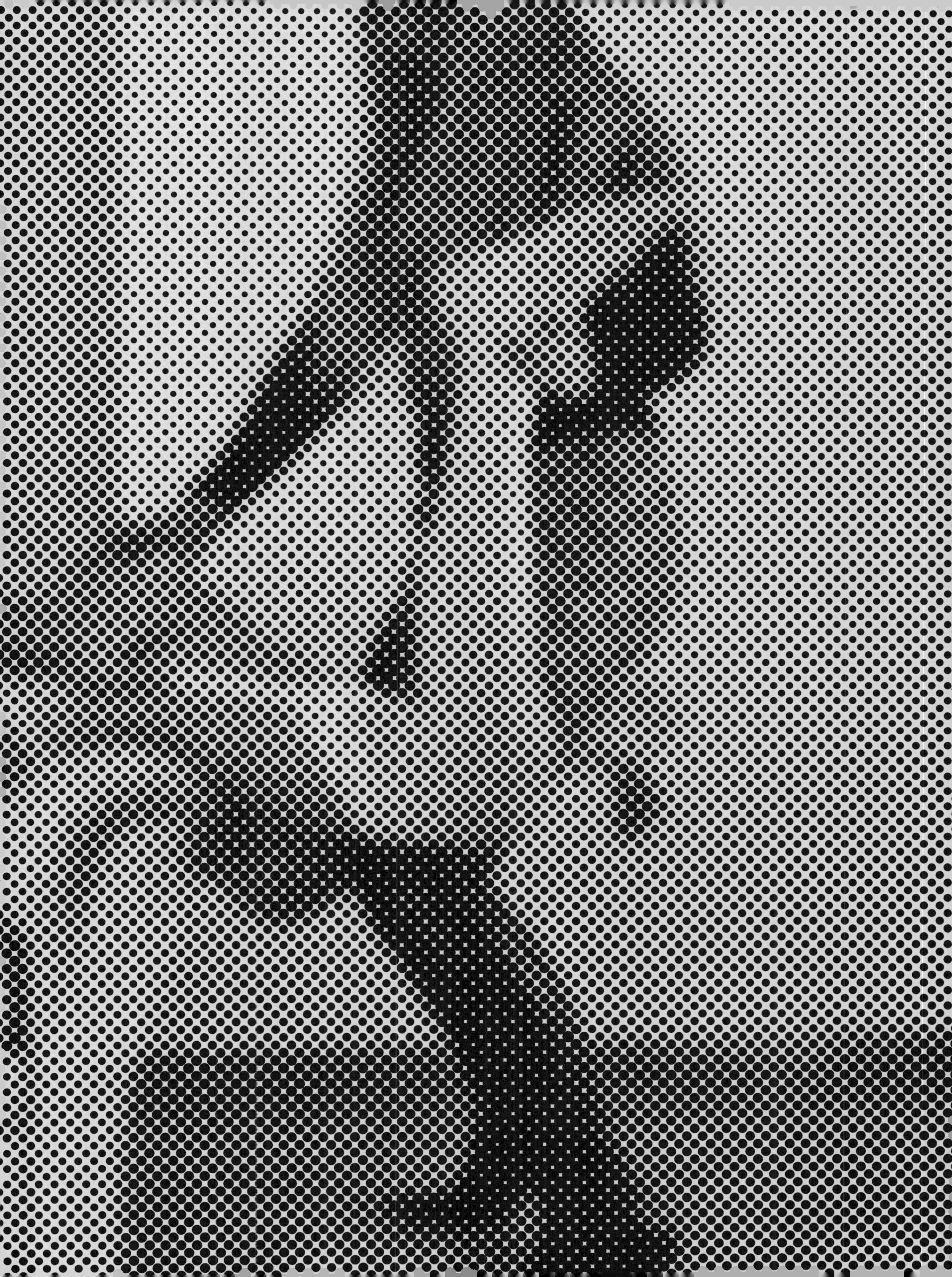

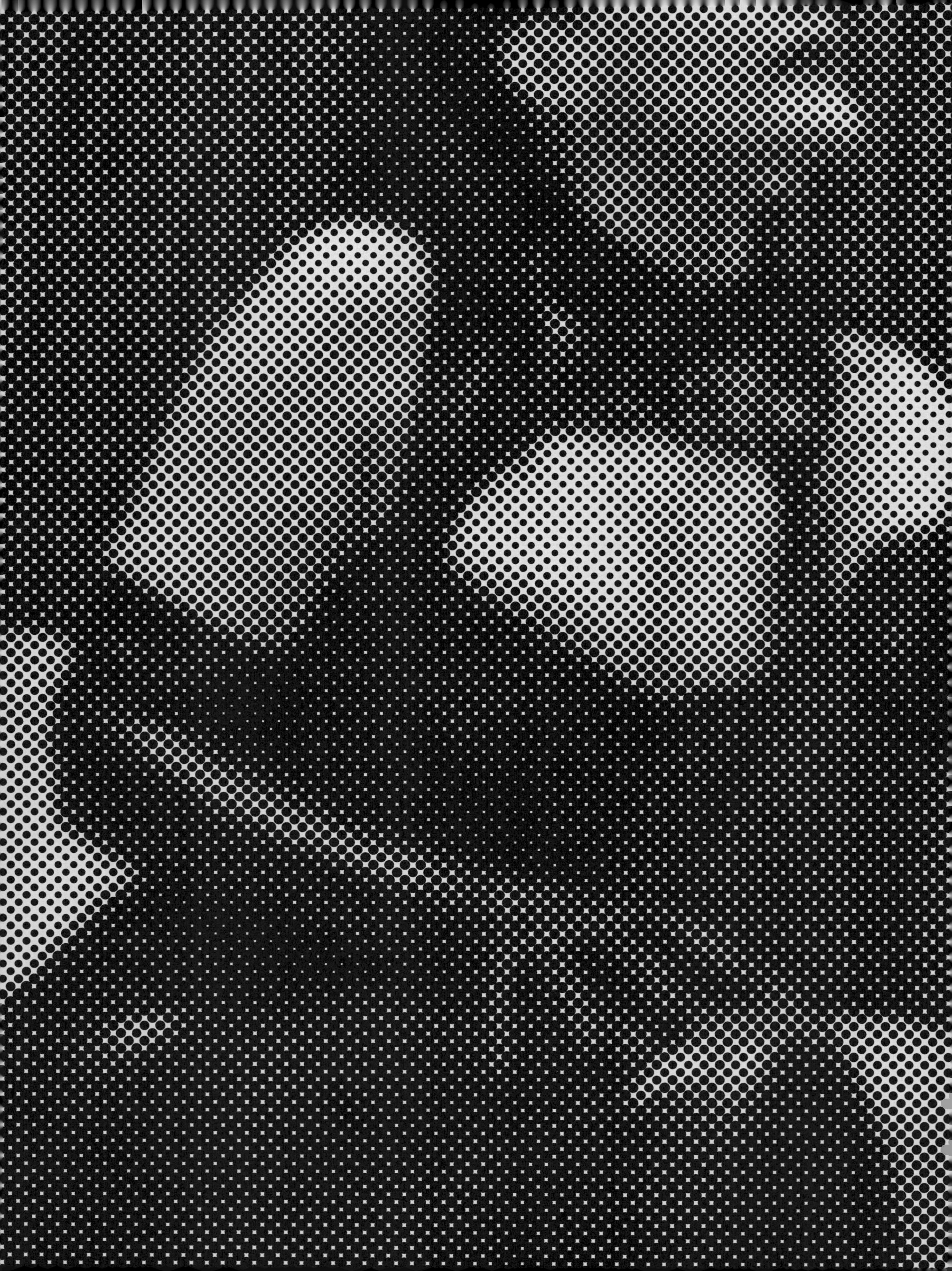

‘For me, there is nothing more natural than living out these desires. That’s just the way it is. It’s a part of you that you can’t deny.’

‘Many guests are ashamed because of their desires. I find that sad, because it’s nothing to be ashamed of. Shame doesn’t exist for me.’

‘Our guests are, of course, mostly men. But couples are becoming more frequent – to pep up their sex lives, I guess. I could also do it with a woman. But that doesn’t happen. Those who want it get it for free; they don’t have to pay for it. There are also many more younger guests. It wasn’t that way earlier; there were only older guests. But now younger ones are coming as well. It’s not only S&M anymore, but bizarre things are also being demanded. Through the Internet, the offers for certain sexual interests have become so widespread and easily accessible that you need to find a new kick, and this is where this “perverse” stuff comes in – and it’s especially the young people who ask for this.’

‘It’s not about the individual act; it’s not about wearing leather or latex or holding a whip, but rather, in principle, about actually feeling yourself, about connecting with yourself. At that moment, when you break away from this pattern – cuddling, kissing, sex, sleeping – and allow even some kind of playful act to take place, regardless of what it is, that’s where S&M actually begins.’

‘Within the dominatrix there’s a person who’s fully dedicated to herself and gives herself up completely and says: So, I’ll guide you now and make sure you feel incredibly good and completely aroused and can just be yourself, who you really are. We’ll get rid of first and last names, get rid of upbringing and influences, get rid of language and everything else that somehow made you who you are. This is a point that you don’t reach in everyday life, the point where you finally find your own self, with moaning, with shaking, with shouting, with whatever. It’s mind-boggling.’

‘Anything can be a fetish – a word, an object. It doesn’t matter.’

‘There are so many more facets than just working towards an orgasm. So much more happens. It’s amazing what goes on in your head. What I feel is less physical; it’s more like a power game, a kind of abandonment, because I get so involved with the other person and can feel how he also just lets himself fall.’

‘Recently, someone brought cake and coffee, and then I spent an hour with him – talking together, drinking coffee and eating cake.’

‘In there, you’re simply naked. I notice within a few minutes whether the desire is real or if it’s fake.’

‘The libidinous lust began with uniforms. Seeing uniforms always made me horny. This authority – on others, as well as on myself! It simply gave me great sensual pleasure. Already at 16, I guess, or sometime around then. And all this black leather, these whips, this darkness and the mystery, the whole mood: It was like being a little high, and I wanted to experience this sensation more intensely. This feeling of intoxication continues to this day.’

‘It’s not about them going to a dominatrix, but rather about them going to someone who can fulfil their desires – that’s the point.’

‘I couldn’t simply give it up. If I were to stop working, I would probably start going to fetish parties again.’

‘How can you imagine that you’re a pig and about to be slaughtered? I don’t understand it; I’ll never understand it. Where’s the eroticism? But I offer it anyway, of course! You have to make a living somehow.’

‘Anyone looking from the outside who saw you in the middle of an S&M act that he doesn’t understand, would say: “That’s inhuman.” But those who experience themselves open themselves up and are understood; they can then show what they’re feeling right now and what’s happening with them, and show that it touches them.’

‘A fantasy is played out. The outfit is part of the scenery.’

‘I have one client who works hard all week and has a second job on the weekend. A house, three children, a wife. He loves her and he loves his children. But he has no sex at home; there’s nothing going on between the sheets anymore. But despite all this, he puts up with everything and works himself half to death so that everyone has what they want and need, so that no one misses out on anything. Now he goes every three months to an S&M studio, looks for compensation, basically charges up his battery again, lets himself go. If he told his wife, she’d divorce him immediately. She would immediately call everything into question: his love, his role as a father, his care, her trust, everything. She’d question everything, merely because he pursued a need that she neglected. Ultimately, she would demand that her loving husband, who does everything for her and their three children, should in any event forgo his own needs just so that she is not offended. I call that egoistic and small-minded.’

‘My fetish is the human psyche.’

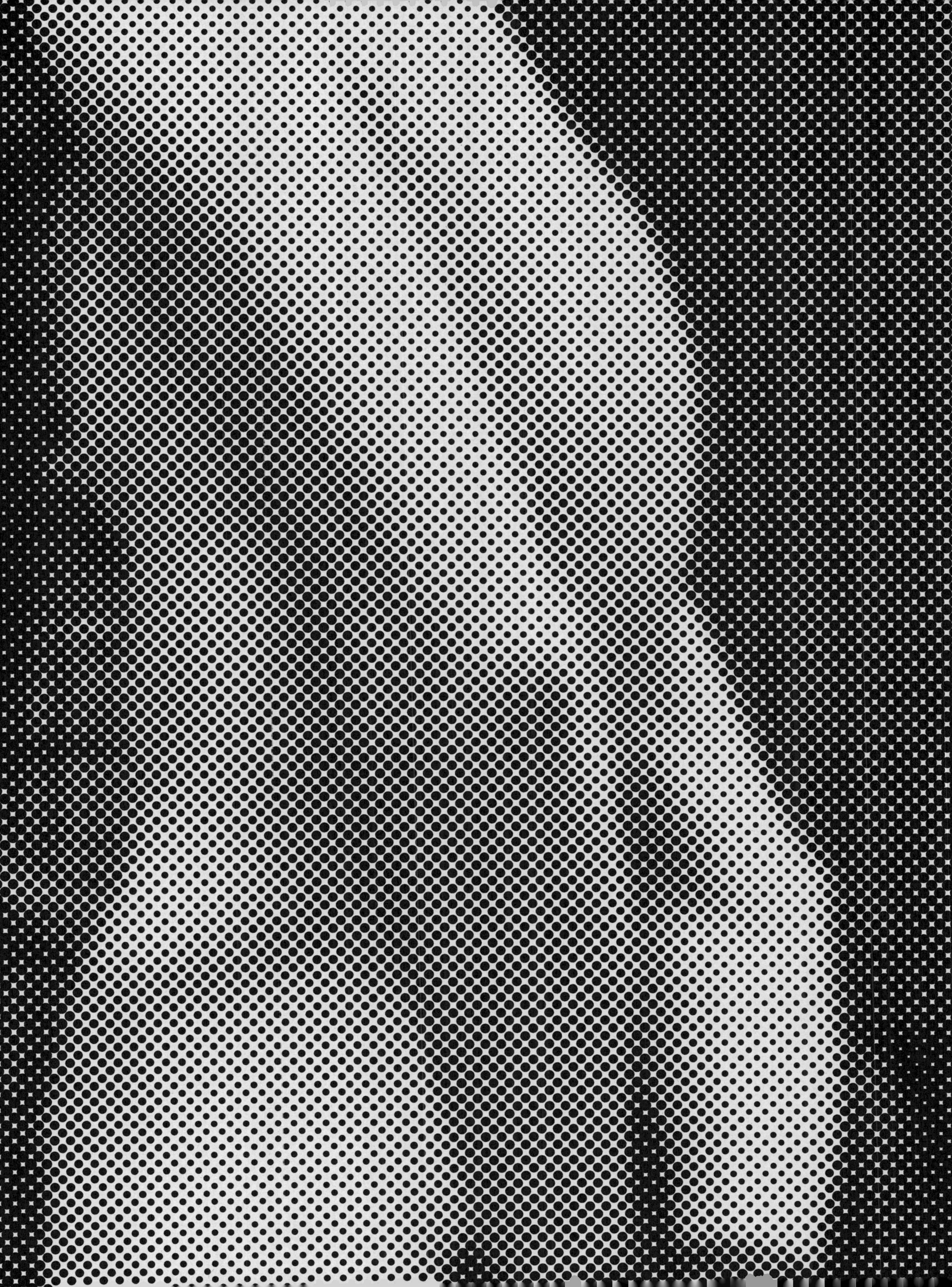

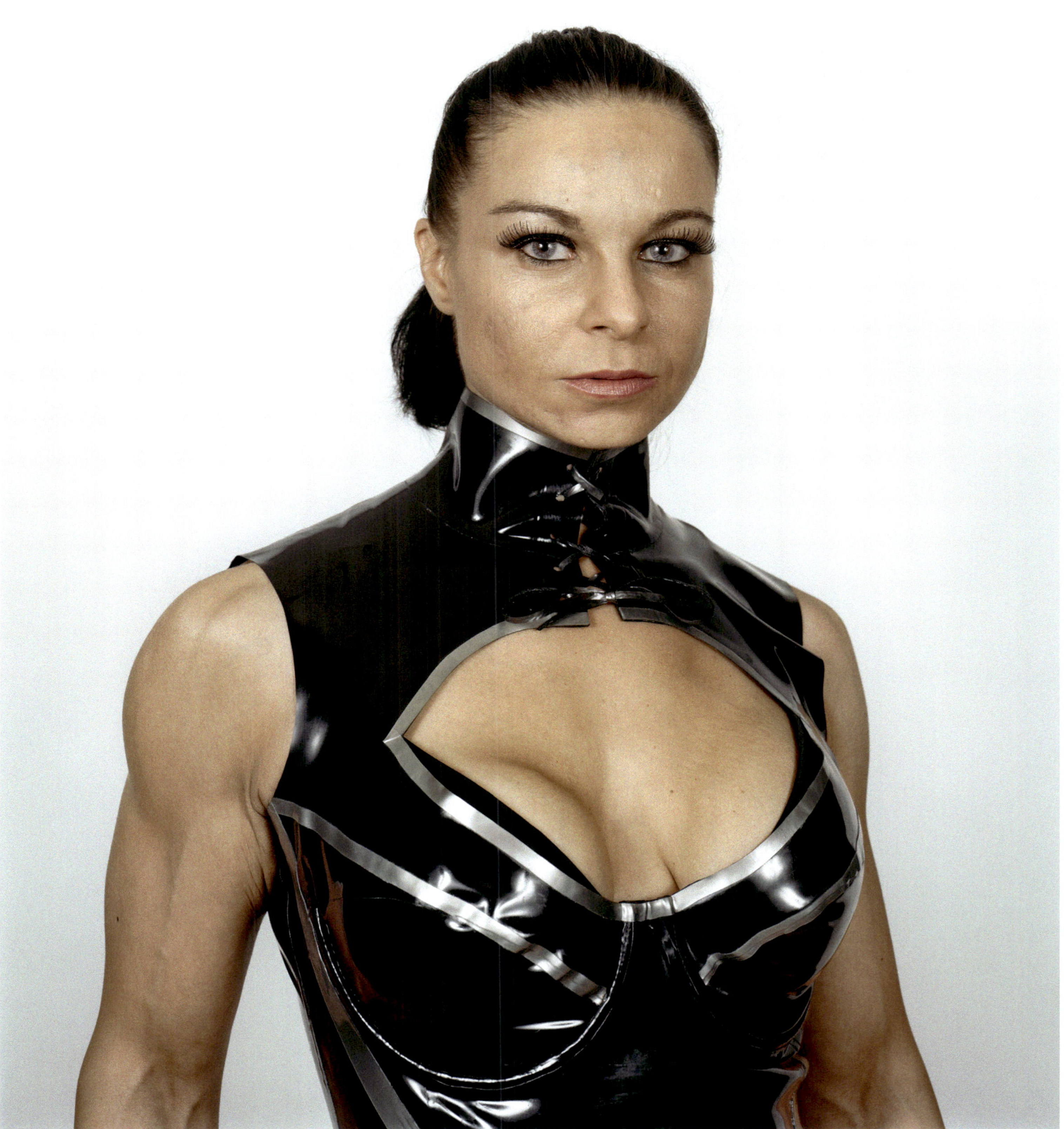

LADY SILVER · Munich, 2016

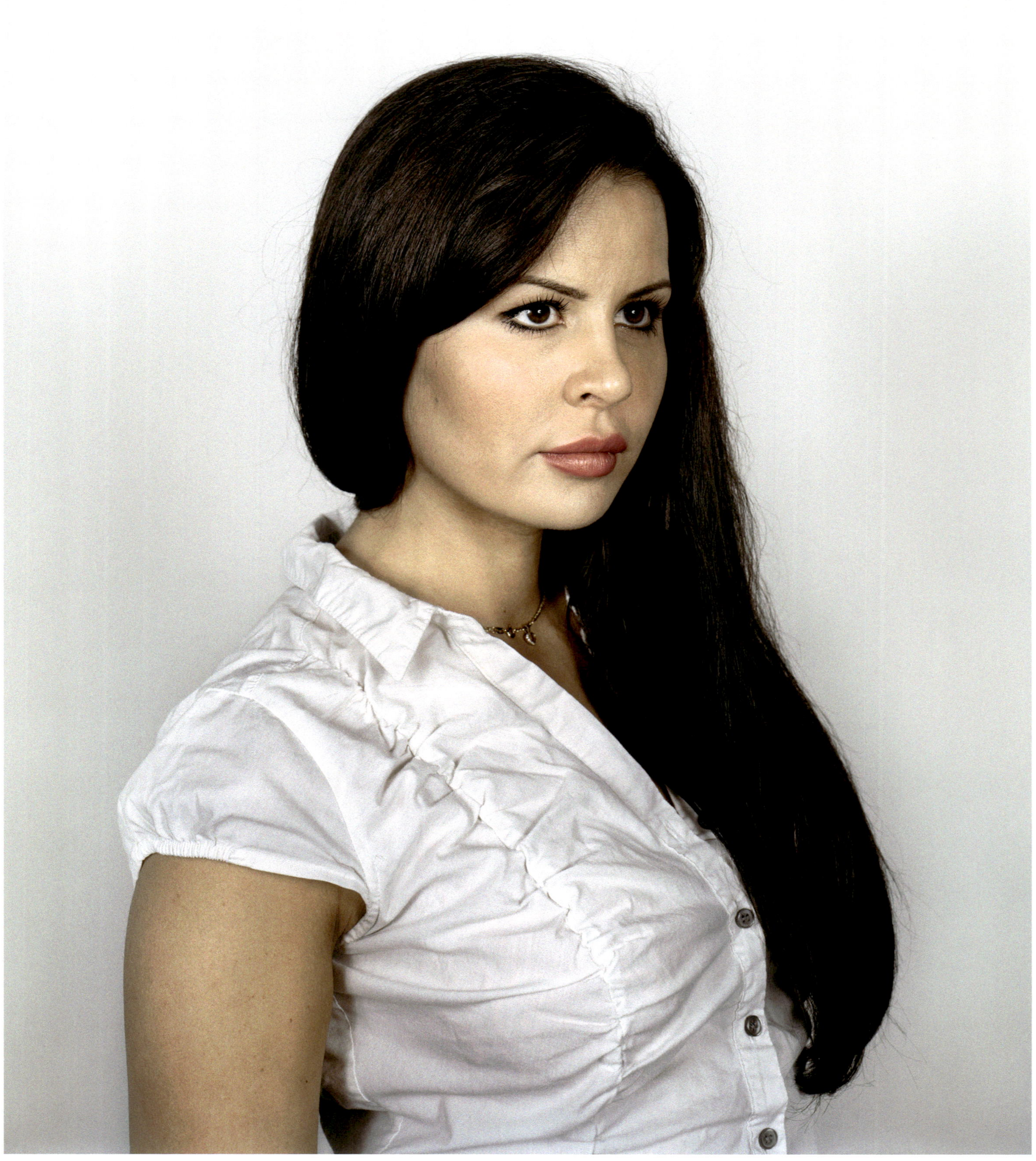

LADY LANA · Frankfurt, 2016

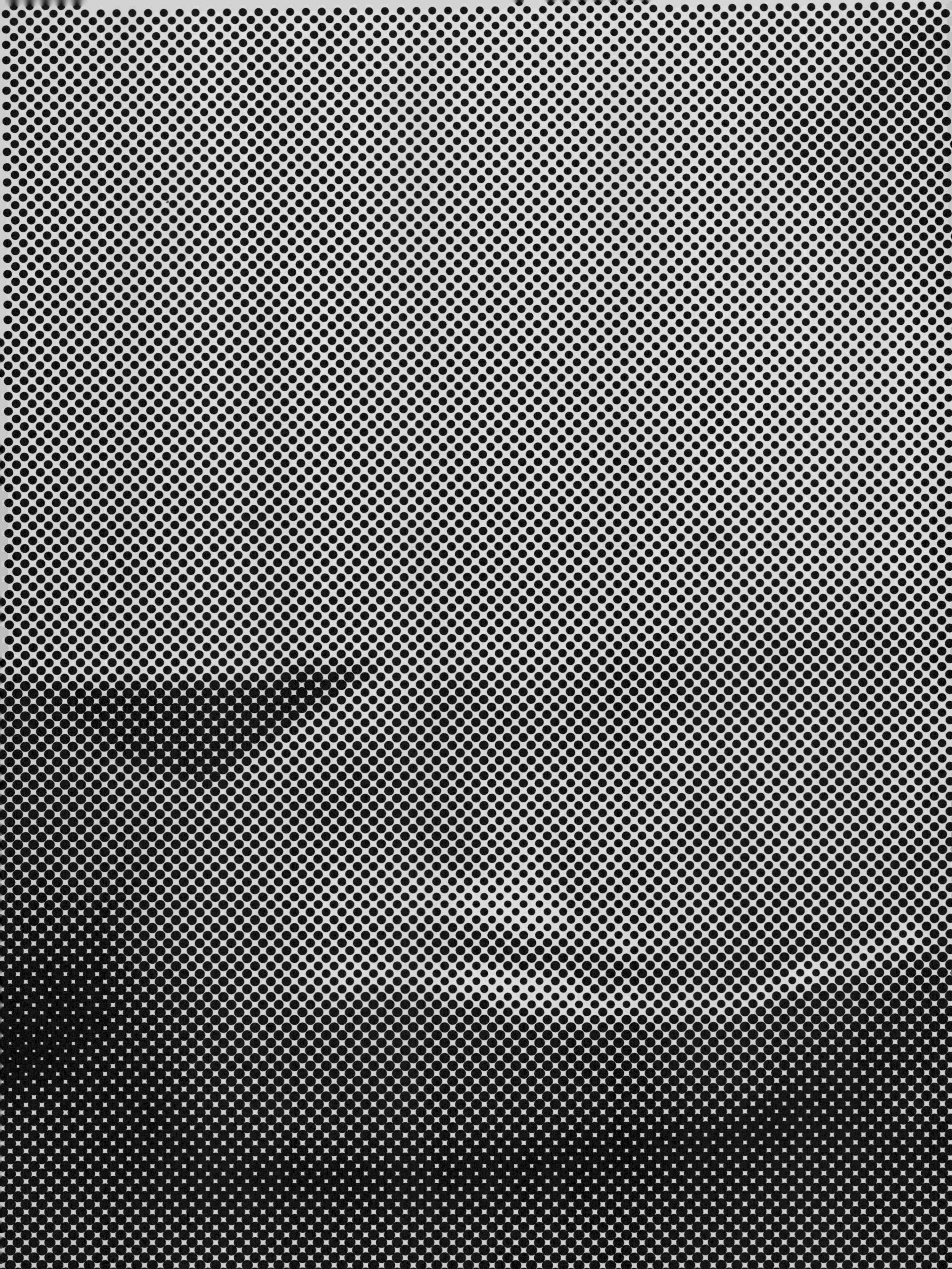

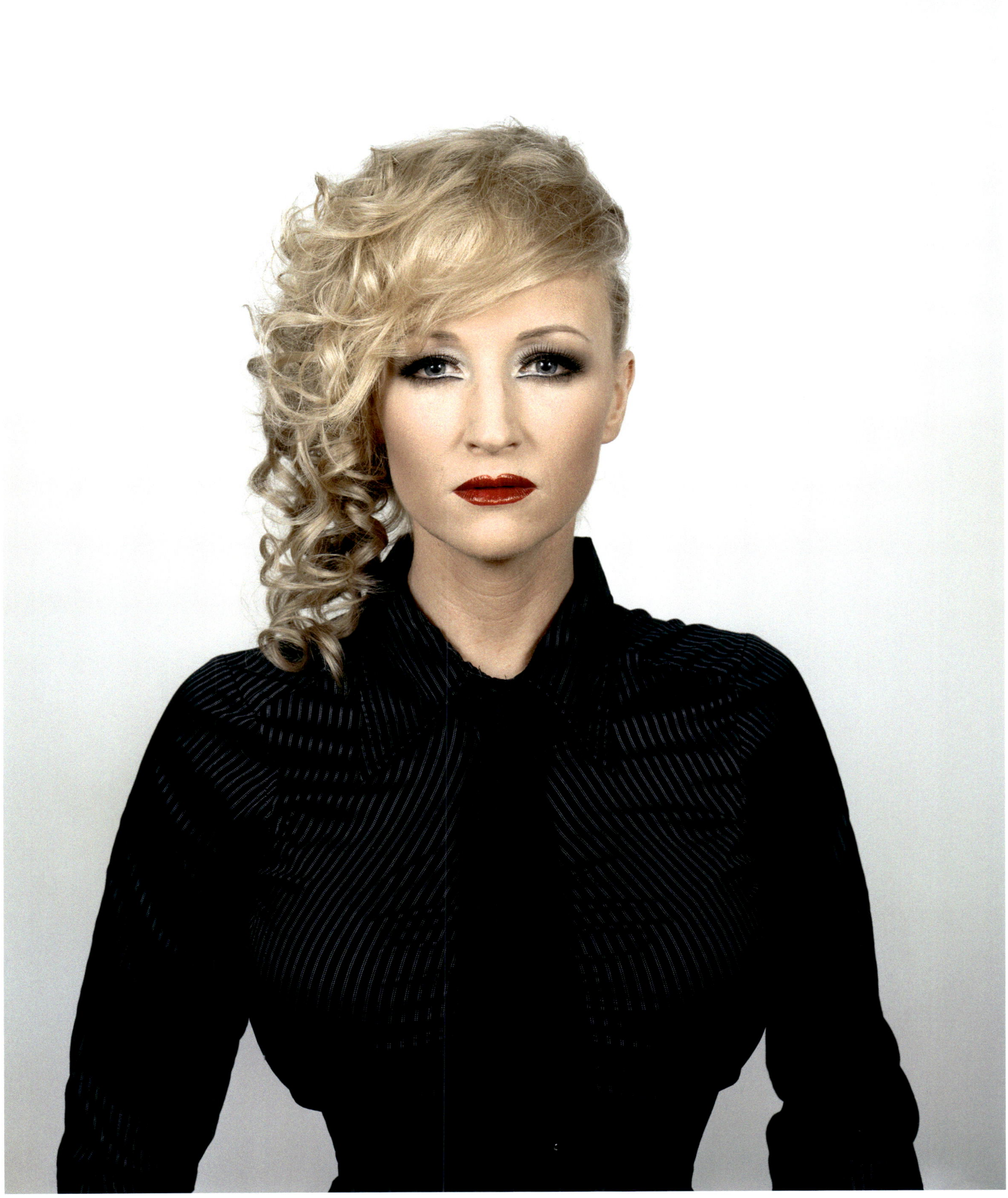

MISS PEEL · Cologne, 2013

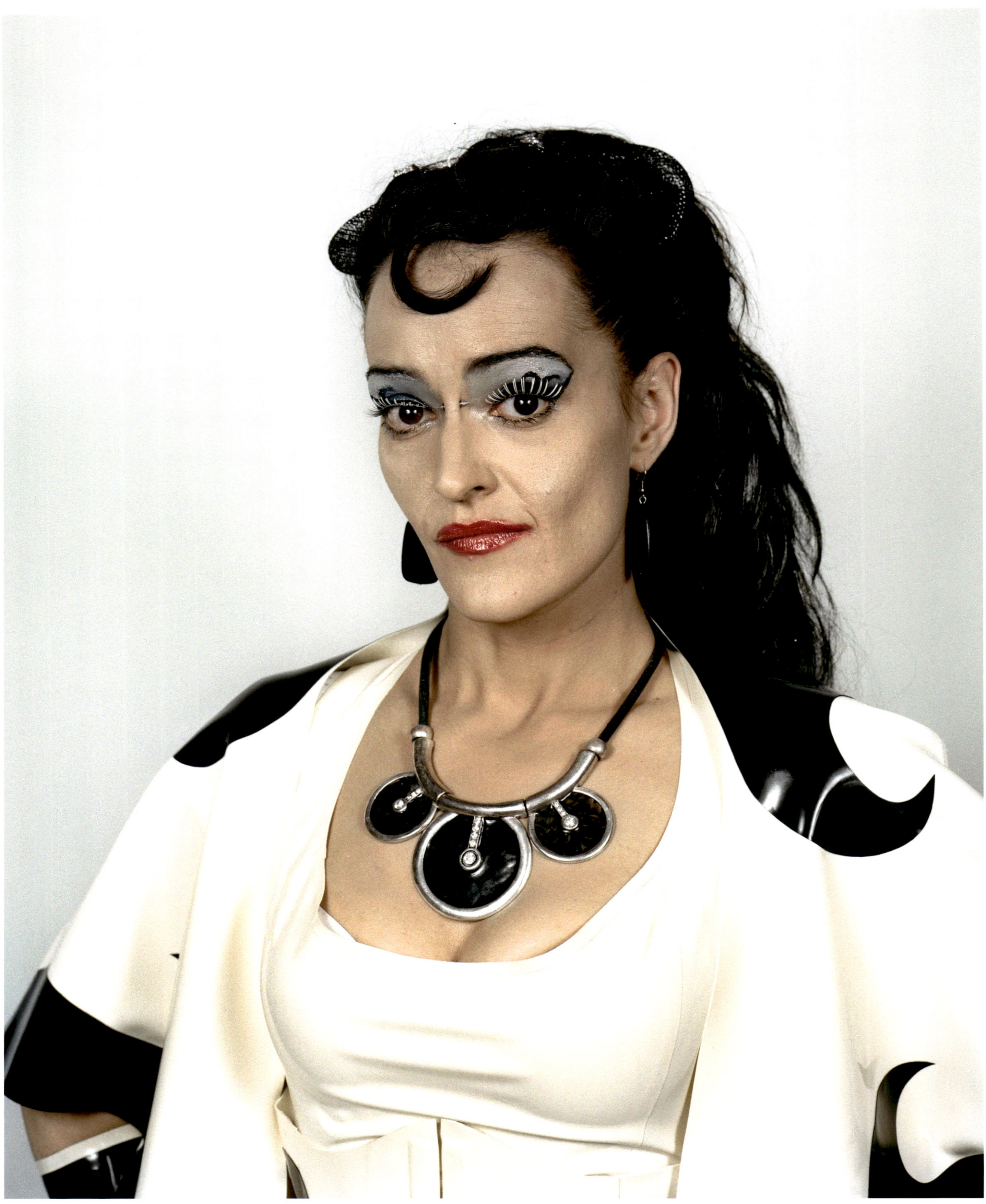

LADY XARA · Berlin, 2013

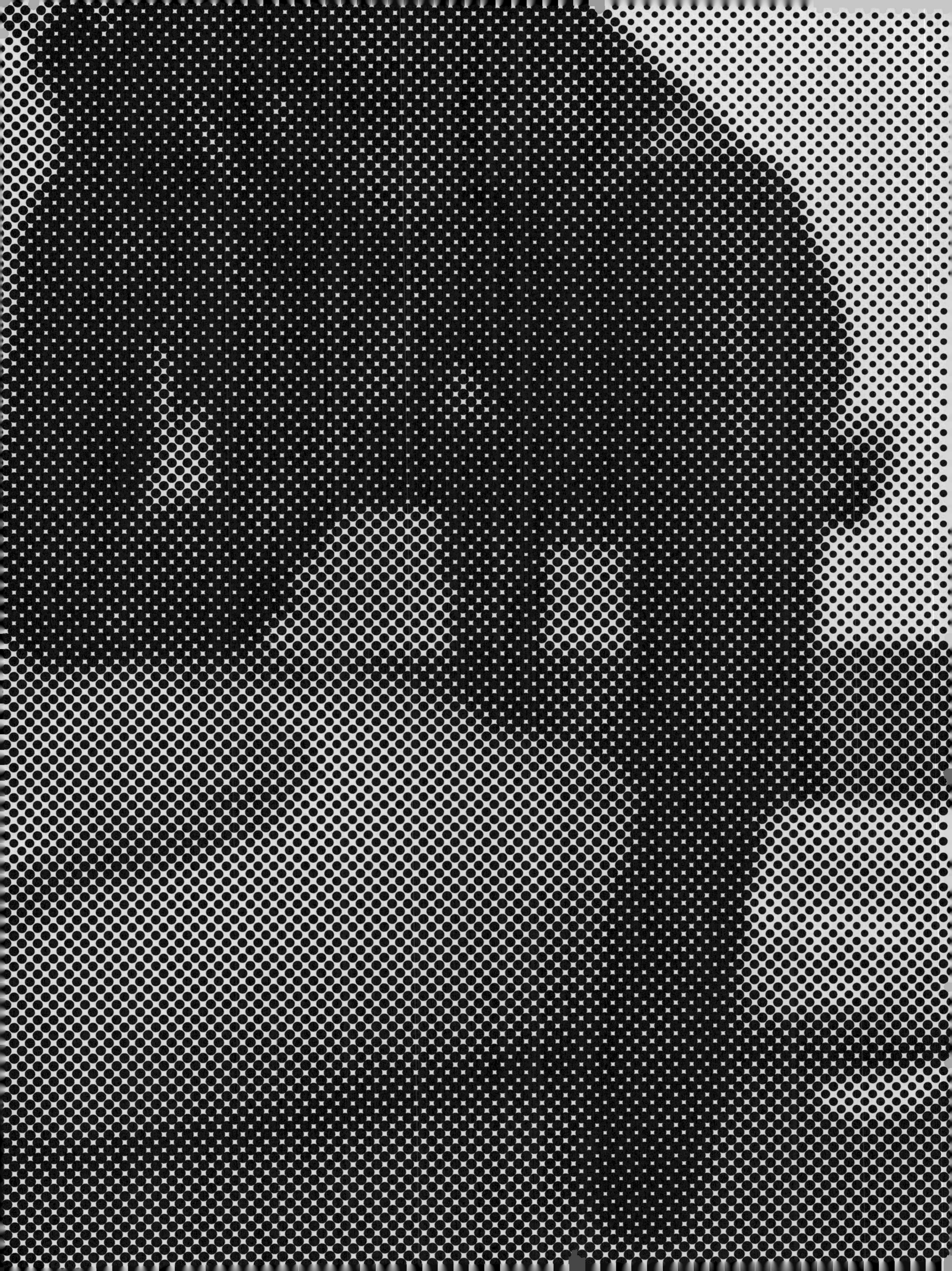

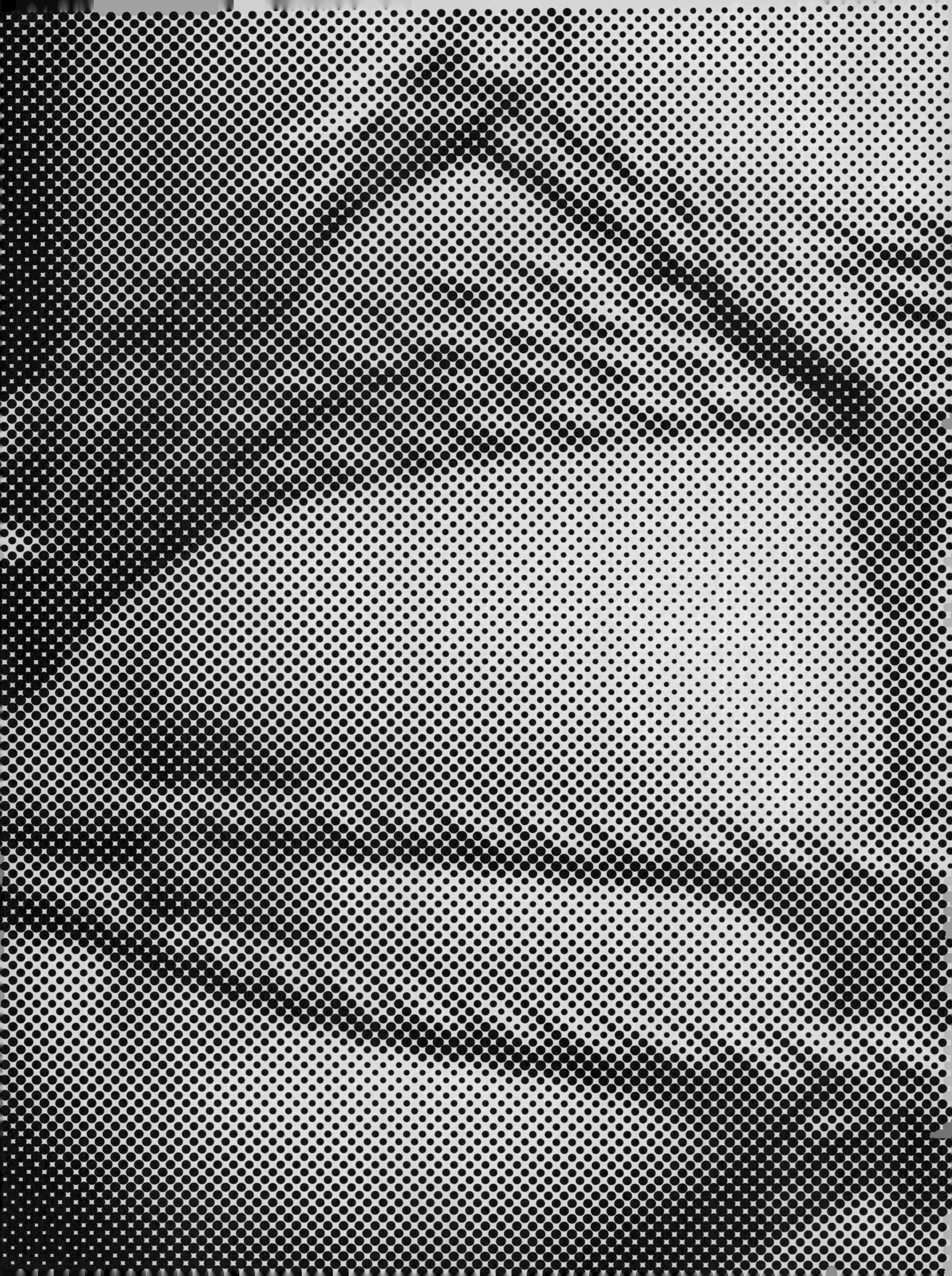

‘You have to be aware of the fact that you now live outside normal conventions. A fellow student found out that I work as a dominatrix and wrote to me asking if I had really thought about the consequences of my “side job”, because it was already the main topic of the entire semester. For the first time, I was afraid of going to the uni. And then I listened time and again to the song “Lasse redn” (“Let them talk”) by “Die Ärzte”.’

‘My mother snooped around a bit, and that was really dreadful. For almost a year, we had absolutely no contact, and it was two or three years before we were able to talk things out.’

‘I’m tougher now; I find myself beautiful – I didn’t find myself beautiful before. I’ve cooled down. Speaking of everyday problems: Things don’t make me upset as quickly as they do with other women. Someone has to practically die before I start getting shaken up.’

‘The price I pay? Loneliness. Few are happy. The difficult thing is the connection to your private life. It’s true that you miss out on your own life. Weeks and months go by – and you’re still sitting in the same spot.’

‘Those I count among my circle of friends have already passed the test of courage of wanting to become friends with me.’

‘At home, I’m completely submissive. I cook and I clean. It feels right. I want to love my husband, of course, especially when he fulfils my every wish. But out there I’m a real “hard shell – soft core” type and more the active, dominant sadist.’

‘My children don’t know that I’m a dominatrix. They think that I’m a model, and I want them to continue thinking this until the time comes when they’re old enough and have the mental maturity to take it all in. I stand behind my job; I feed them with it. They live a good life and I can always be there for them, because I don’t have a nine-to-five job. I’m a single mother; I’m not constantly annoyed and irritated. I can really be there for them.’

‘No one can tell me that you can do this job without it having an effect on you, without it doing something to you. For my part, it made me grow up very quickly.’

‘I met my current companion as a guest. In business, they say that boundaries are extremely important, which, in principle, is actually quite reasonable. But when it happens, then it happens. For me, it had a lot of advantages. I didn’t have to justify myself because of my job. My partner accepts my job. We deal with it very openly. I think that this kind of acceptance is only possible with someone who knows a lot about the topic.’

‘No, I could never fall in love with a guest, because I would always see him as a guest. A guest remains a guest. Never mix the professional with the private.’

‘When I go home after an appointment, I want to put it all behind me. I don’t want to see the damned high heels; I don’t want to see any nylons. I want to have a completely normal person next to me, no damned whips and no gasmasks. Most dominatrices are actually quite submissive in their private lives. When you fulfil desires the whole time as part of your profession, you want to just fall into bed and simply let the guy take over.’

‘In the dungeon, there’s so much frustration and alcohol. The guests buy themselves irresponsibility.’

‘You become hostile towards men as a result of the job. It’s already the case that I don’t meet up with men anymore outside of work. You’re simply taken advantage of. The biggest arse in the dungeon gets on my nerves more than you can imagine. But at least he pays for it! But out there – should I let myself be put down by some idiot for nothing?’

‘Life as a dominatrix has strengthened my personality. My self-esteem has gotten much greater. I’ve learned more than I ever imagined, from good small talk to a deeper knowledge of human nature.’

‘Most of the ladies don’t have any friends anymore; it’s very, very, very rare. Partners yes, but friends no, because you’re actually preoccupied with yourself and no longer take any real notice of others. And many don’t handle it very well anyway.’

‘Strength means being able to stand up and say, I am not a stereotype. I am myself. And this is actually something that I wish for everyone.’

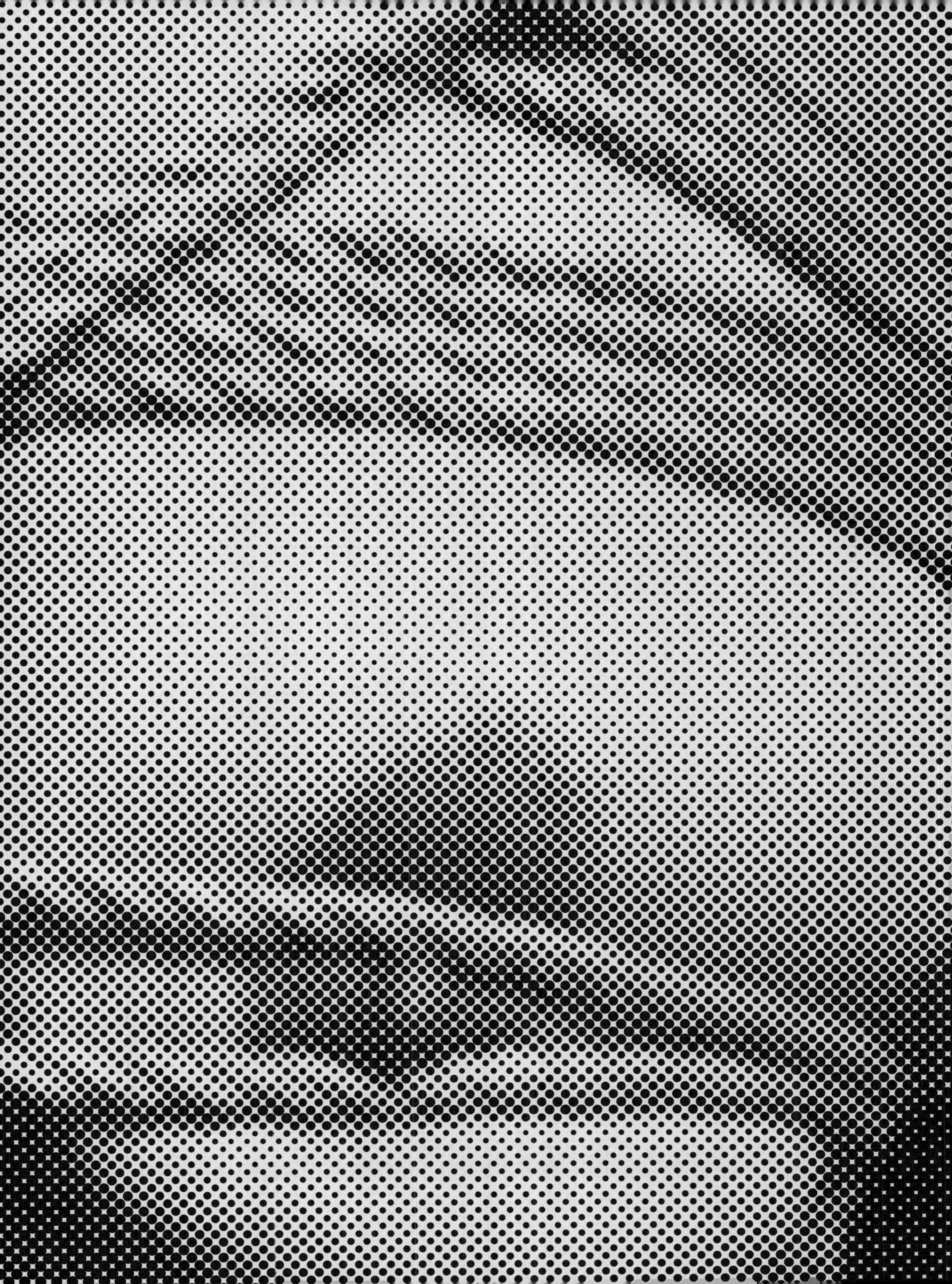

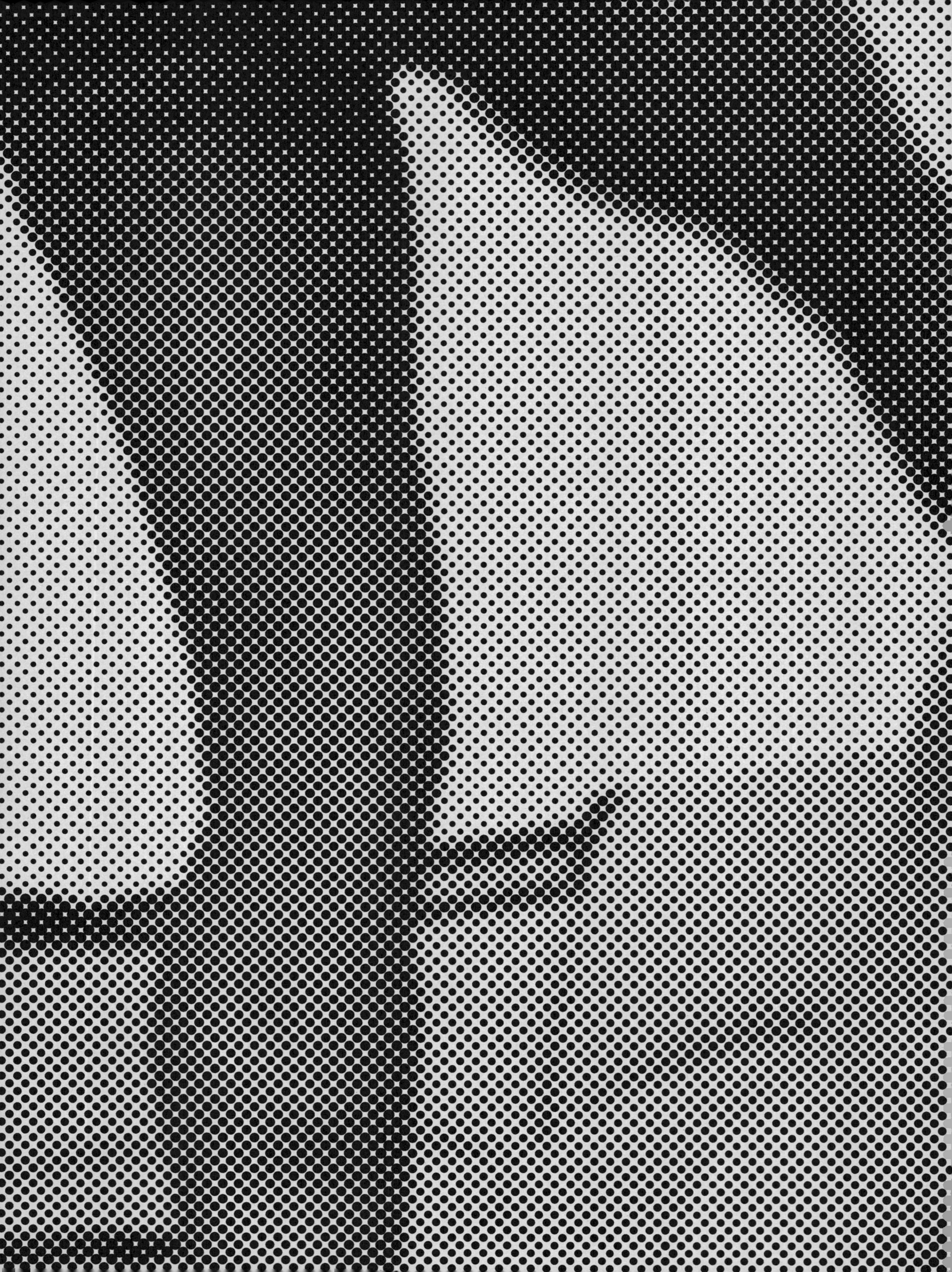

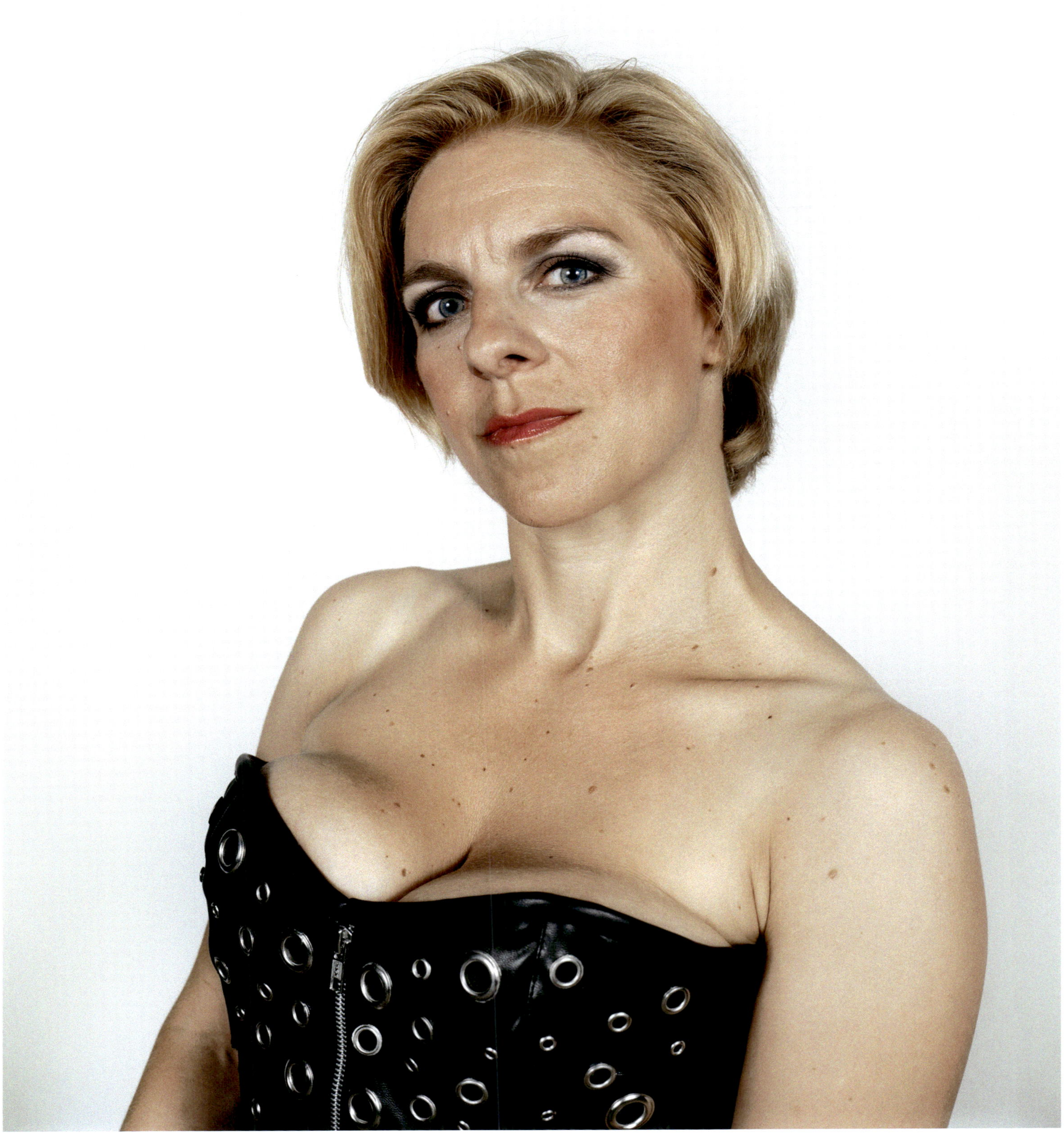

FRÄULEIN SCHMITT · Berlin, 2013

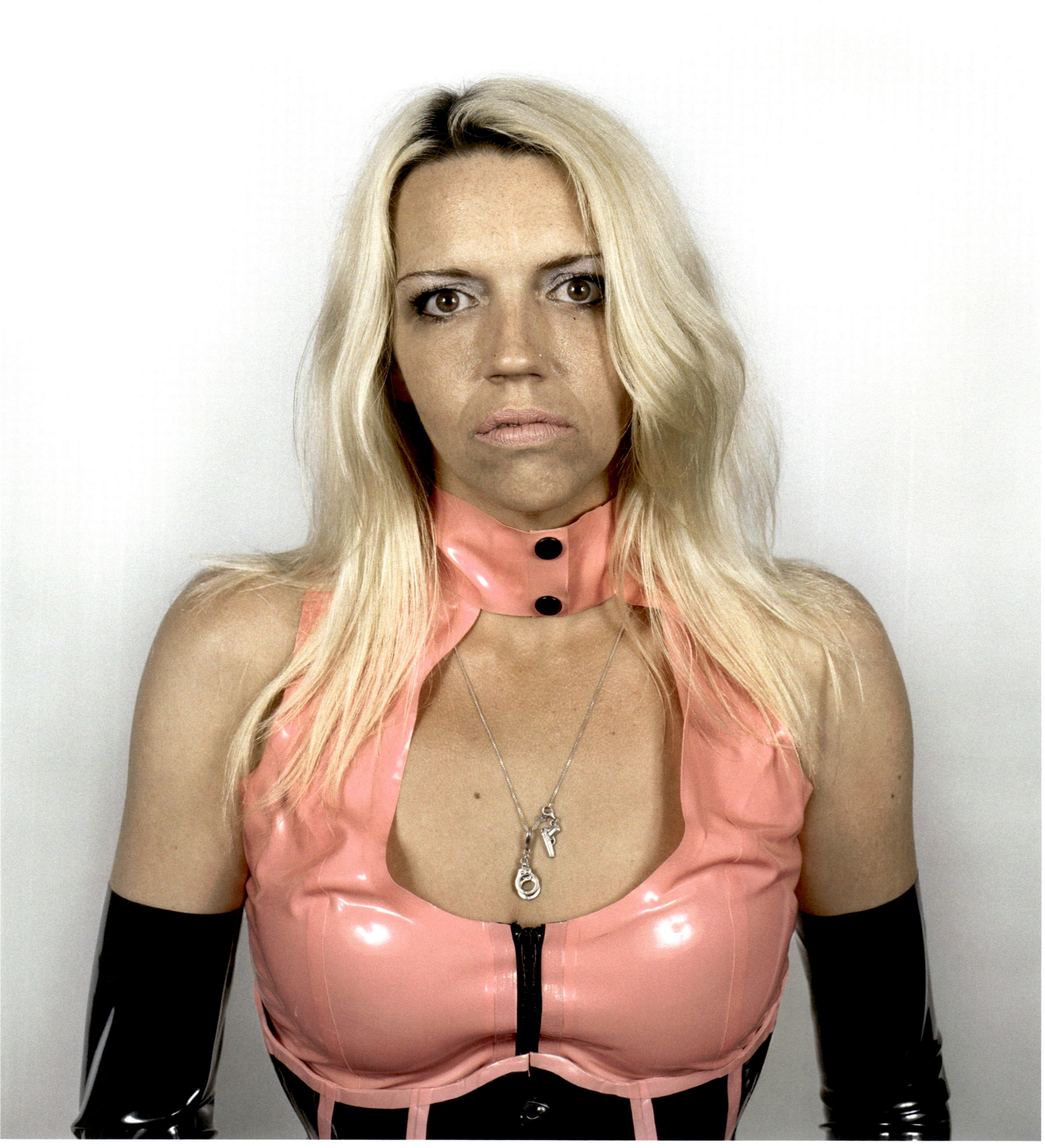

LADY STEFANIE · Stuttgart, 2016

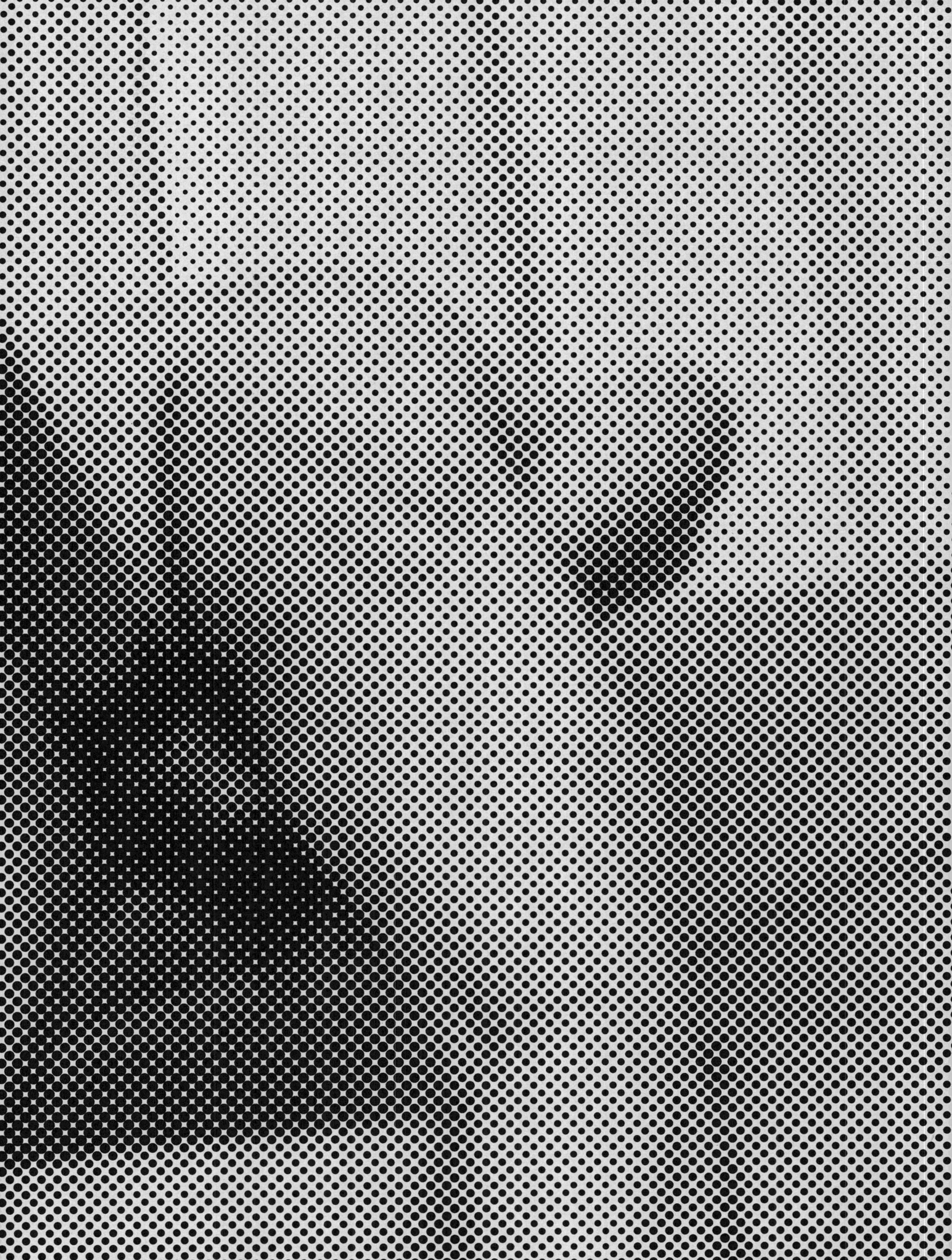

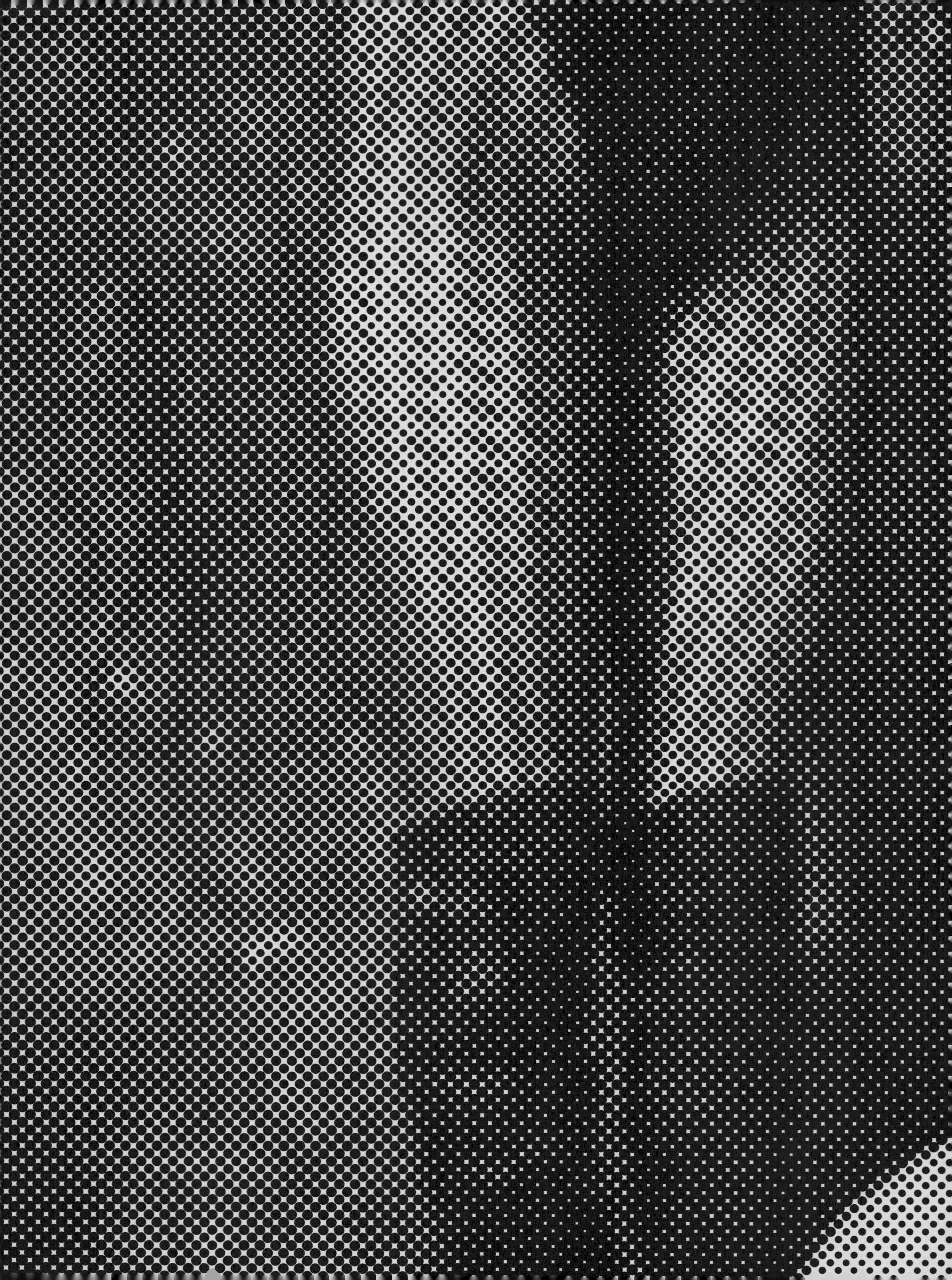

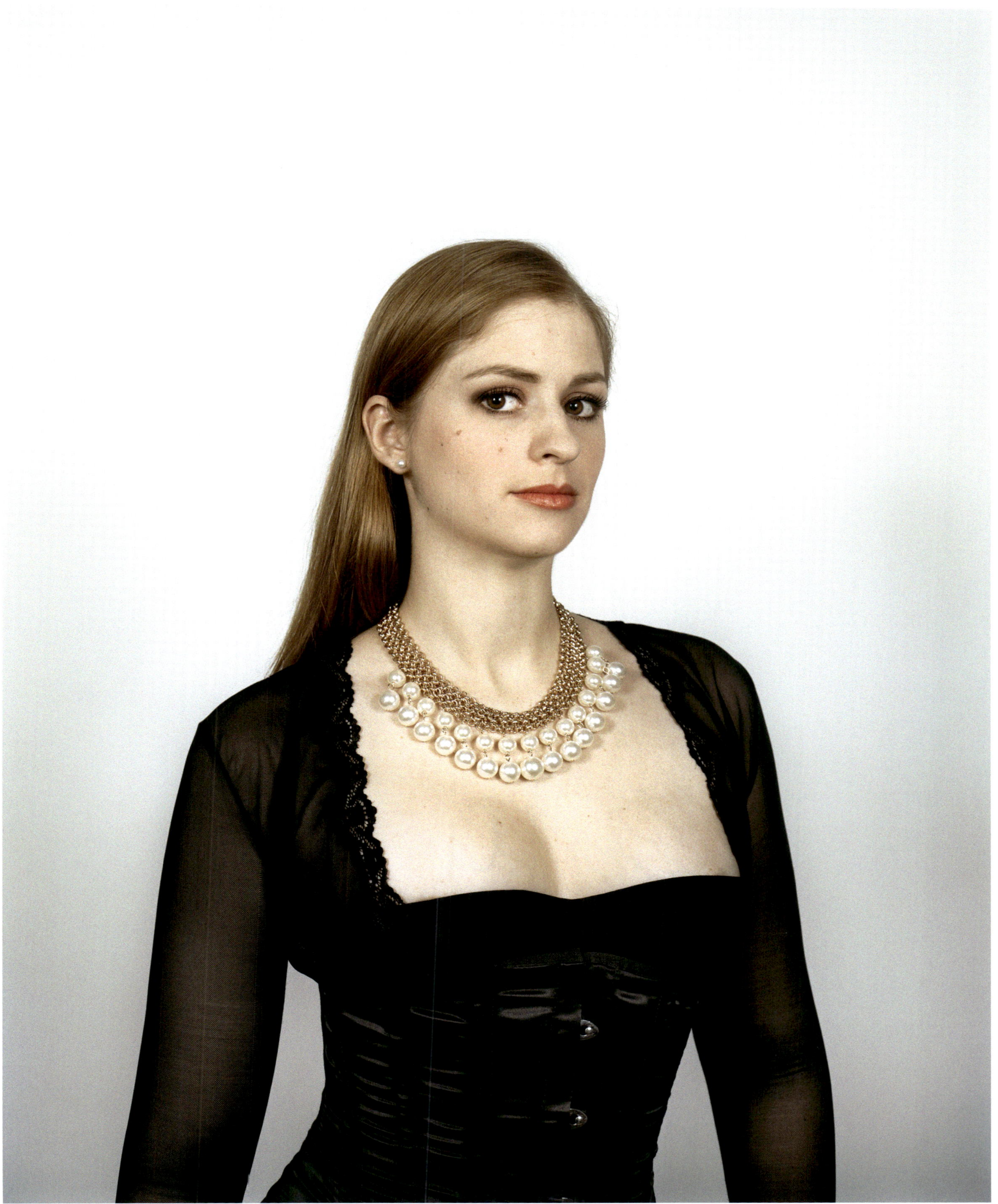

BIZARRLADY AMY · Berlin, 2014

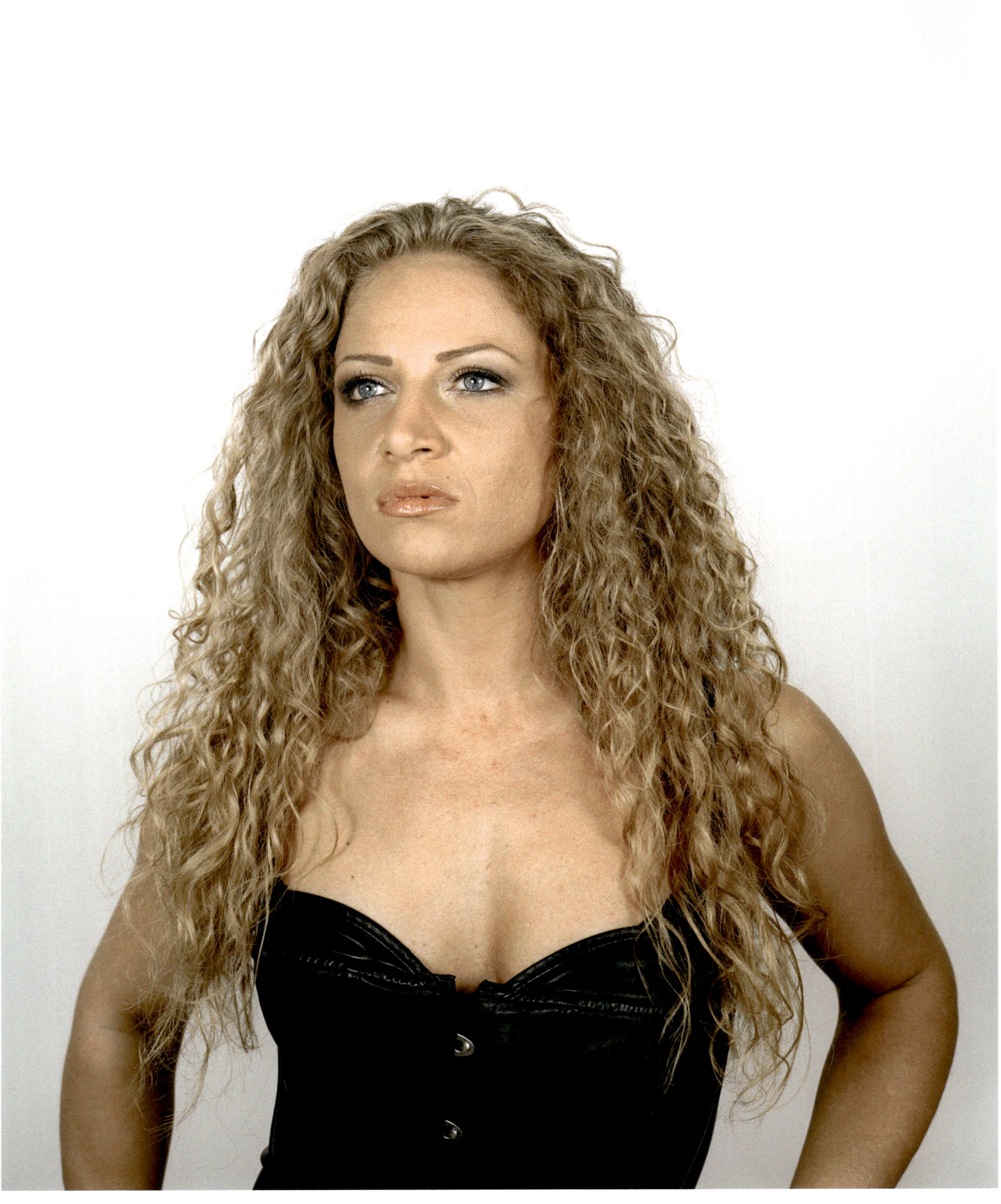

LADY DESTINY DARK · Munich, 2013

ACKNOWLEDGEMENTS

I would especially like to thank all the women who let me portray them as part of this project. It has been a great honour to get to know you and photograph you. I thank you for your trust, your time, your suggestions, the new connections, and the numerous conversations. I would also like to thank the women who decided against taking part in this project, a decision that I deeply respect.

Many thanks also to the following people: Simone Albiez, Agnes Bachmaier, Christoph Bangert, Alexa Becker, Adam Broomberg, Alice Bucknell, Oliver Chanarin, Erik Clewe, Selina Dieter, Sarah Doerfel, Gerhild Eicke, Sigrid Eicke-Illmer, Nina Faulhaber, Lisa-Katharina Förster, Gérard A. Goodrow, Klaus Grittner, Luzi Gross, Marius W Hansen, Grey Hutton, Barbara Karpf, Klaus Kehrer, Karin Kontny, Andreas Kronawitt, Martin Lutz, Lou Miller, Dorrit Nebe, Renate Niebler, Robin Rehm, Anthony Santoro, Tobias Schmitz, Andreas Schubert, Daniel Sommer, Alexander Stöckle, Kathrin Szymikowski, Laura Thiesbrummel, Andreas Trampe, Marion Trenkler, Cedric Vilim, Matthias Wachter, Lars Wittmaak, and Eckhard Wulf.

PHOTOGRAPHS
AND INTERVIEWS
Max Eicke

TEXT EDITING
Lisa-Katharina Förster,
Karin Kontny

COPY EDITING
Anthony Santoro

TRANSLATION
Gérard A. Goodrow

DESIGN
Cedric Vilim

ARTWORK
recom,
Marion Trenkler

IMAGE PROCESSING
Kehrer Design Heidelberg

PRODUCTION
Kehrer Design Heidelberg

With the kind support of

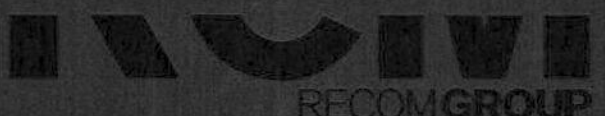

'Dominas' was realised by Max Eicke in Germany and the UK between 2013 and 2016. The text component contains the anonymised statements of the interviewed women. The found footage was appropriated from various online sources.

First edition 2016

Printed and bound in Germany
ISBN 978-3-86828-746-2

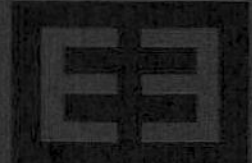

Kehrer Heidelberg Berlin
www.kehrerverlag.com

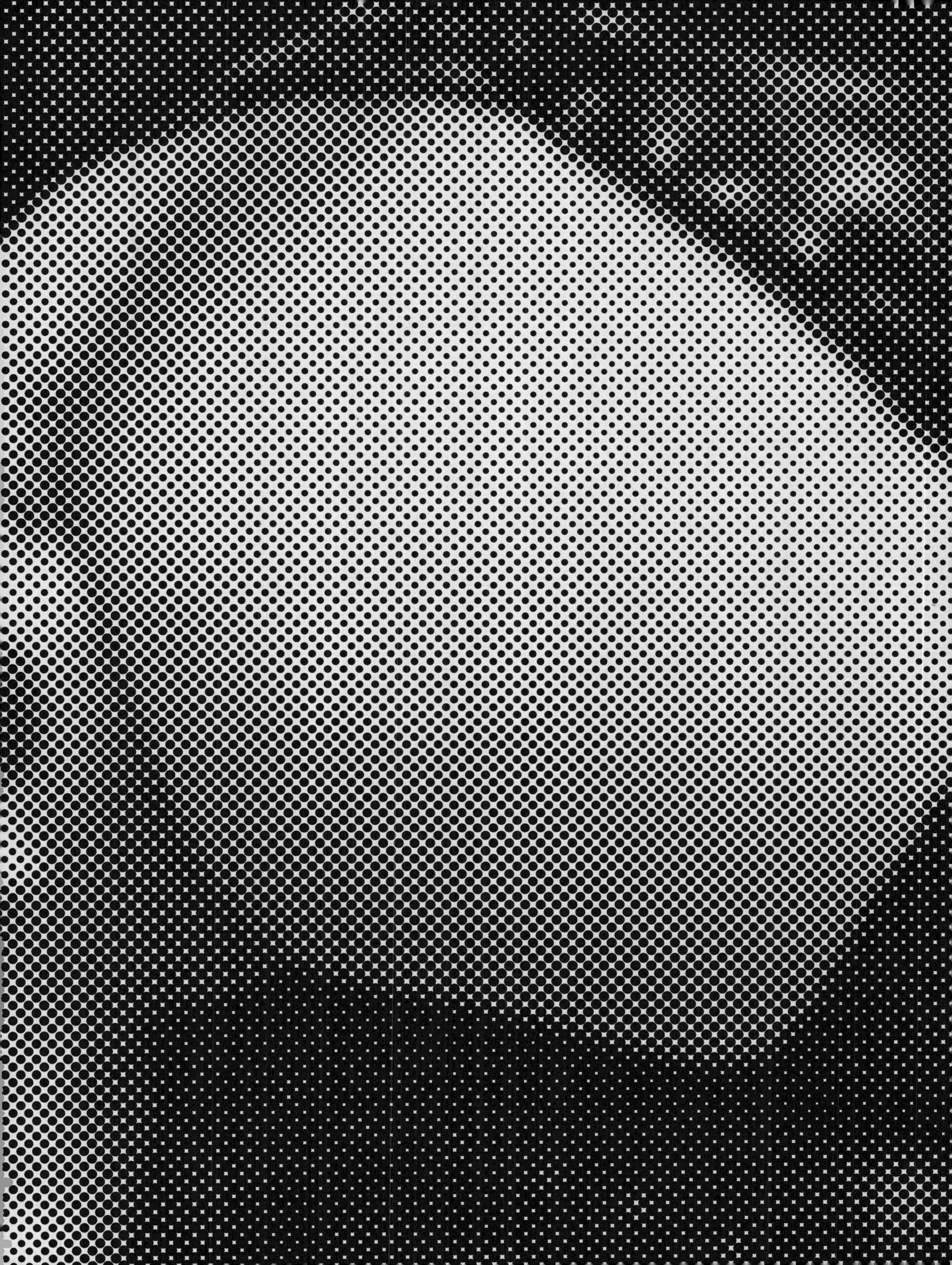

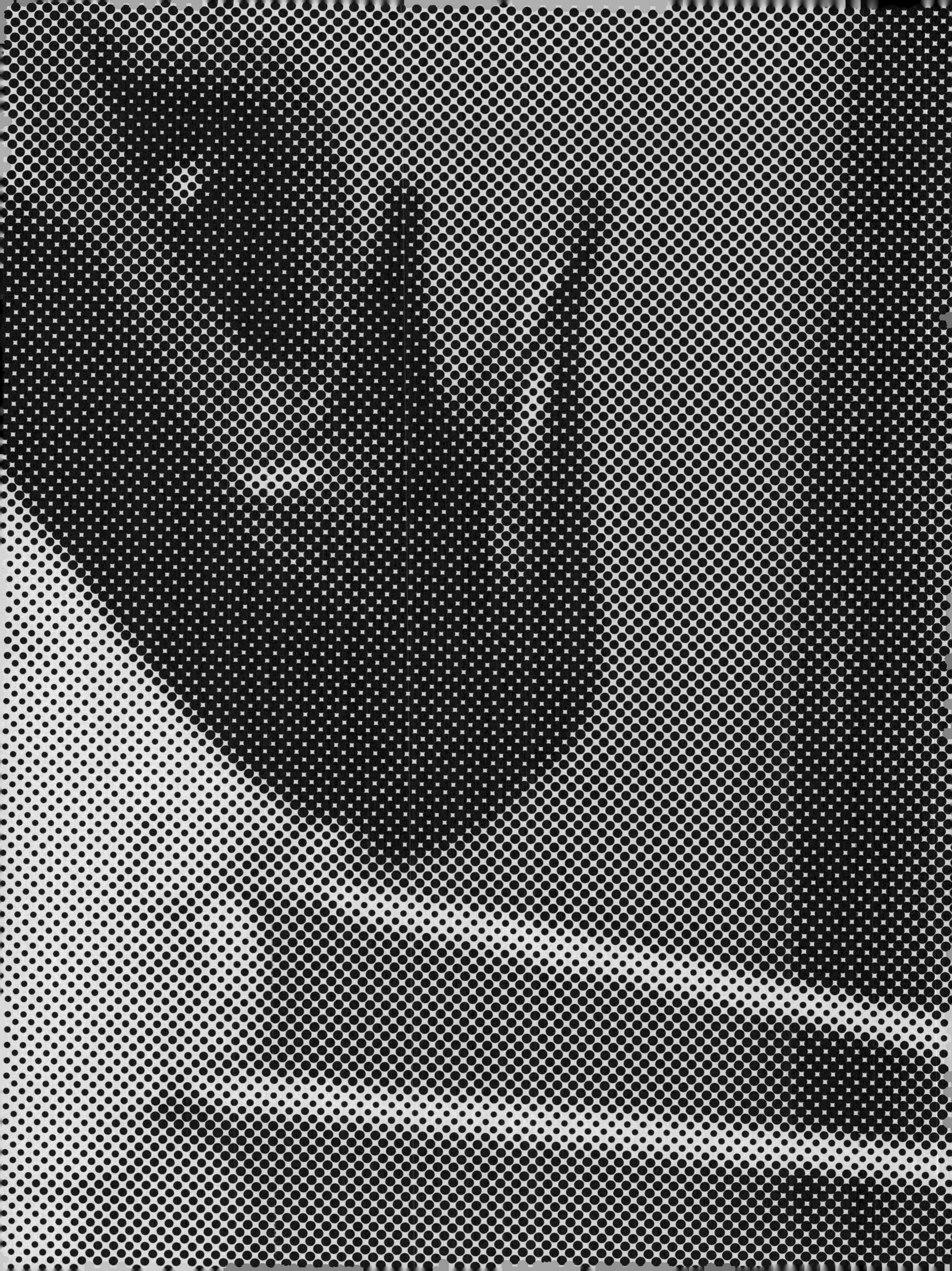

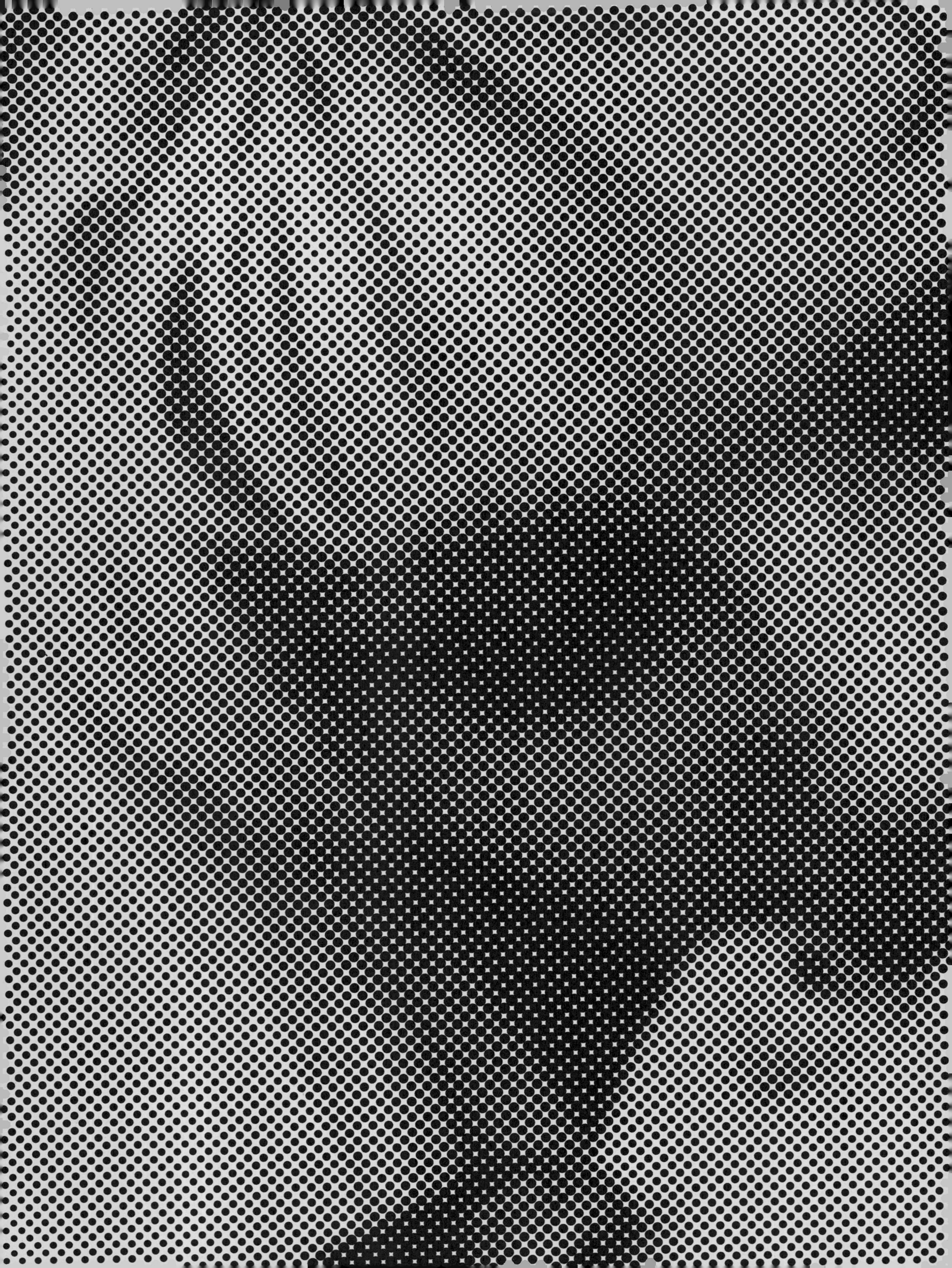